RONALD McNAIR

RONALD McNAIR

Corinne Naden

Senior Consulting Editor
Nathan Irvin Huggins

Director
W.E.B. Du Bois Institute for Afro-American Research
Harvard University

CHELSEA HOUSE PUBLISHERS
New York   Philadelphia

Chelsea House Publishers
Editor-in-Chief Remmel Nunn
Managing Editor Karyn Gullen Browne
Copy Chief Juliann Barbato
Picture Editor Adrian G. Allen
Art Director Maria Epes
Deputy Copy Chief Mark Rifkin
Assistant Art Director Loraine Machlin
Manufacturing Manager Gerald Levine
Systems Manager Rachel Vigier
Production Manager Joseph Romano
Production Coordinator Marie Claire Cebrián

Black Americans of Achievement
Senior Editor Richard Rennert

Staff for RONALD McNAIR
Text Editor Marian W. Taylor
Copy Editor Brian Sookram
Editorial Assistant Leigh Hope Wood
Picture Researcher Andrea Reithmayr
Designer Ghila Krajzman
Cover Illustration Gregory Baker

5 7 9 8 6 4

Library of Congress Cataloging-in-Publication Data

Naden, Corinne.
  Ronald McNair/Corinne Naden.
    p.   cm.—(Black Americans of achievement)
  Includes bibliographical references and index.
  Summary: A biography of the black astronaut who was part of
the ill-fated Challenger space shuttle mission that exploded after
takeoff in January 1986.
  ISBN 0-7910-1133-X
      0-7910-1158-5 (pbk.)
  1. McNair, Ronald E., 1950–86—Juvenile literature.
2. Astronauts—United States—Biography—Juvenile literature.
3. Afro-American astronauts—United States—Biography—
Juvenile literature. [1. McNair, Ronald E., 1950–86.
2. Astronauts. 3. Afro-Americans—Biography.] I. Title. II.
Series.
TL789.85.M36N34 1990
629.45′0092—dc20   90-36596
[B]   CIP
[92]   AC

Frontispiece: *With Ronald Mc-Nair and six colleagues aboard, the shuttle* Challenger *stands ready for lift-off at Cape Canaveral, Florida, in January 1986.*

CONTENTS

———— ❦ ————

BLACK AMERICANS OF ACHIEVEMENT

RALPH ABERNATHY
civil rights leader

MUHAMMAD ALI
heavyweight champion

RICHARD ALLEN
religious leader and social activist

LOUIS ARMSTRONG
musician

ARTHUR ASHE
tennis great

JOSEPHINE BAKER
entertainer

JAMES BALDWIN
author

BENJAMIN BANNEKER
scientist and mathematician

AMIRI BARAKA
poet and playwright

COUNT BASIE
bandleader and composer

ROMARE BEARDEN
artist

JAMES BECKWOURTH
frontiersman

MARY McLEOD
BETHUNE
educator

BLANCHE BRUCE
politician

RALPH BUNCHE
diplomat

GEORGE WASHINGTON
CARVER
botanist

CHARLES CHESNUTT
author

BILL COSBY
entertainer

PAUL CUFFE
merchant and abolitionist

FATHER DIVINE
religious leader

FREDERICK DOUGLASS
abolitionist editor

CHARLES DREW
physician

W.E.B. DU BOIS
scholar and activist

PAUL LAURENCE DUNBAR
poet

KATHERINE DUNHAM
dancer and choreographer

MARIAN WRIGHT EDELMAN
civil rights leader and lawyer

DUKE ELLINGTON
bandleader and composer

RALPH ELLISON
author

JULIUS ERVING
basketball great

JAMES FARMER
civil rights leader

ELLA FITZGERALD
singer

MARCUS GARVEY
black-nationalist leader

DIZZY GILLESPIE
musician

PRINCE HALL
social reformer

W. C. HANDY
father of the blues

WILLIAM HASTIE
educator and politician

MATTHEW HENSON
explorer

CHESTER HIMES
author

BILLIE HOLIDAY
singer

JOHN HOPE
educator

LENA HORNE
entertainer

LANGSTON HUGHES
poet

ZORA NEALE HURSTON
author

JESSE JACKSON
civil rights leader and politician

JACK JOHNSON
heavyweight champion

JAMES WELDON JOHNSON
author

SCOTT JOPLIN
composer

BARBARA JORDAN
politician

MARTIN LUTHER KING, JR.
civil rights leader

ALAIN LOCKE
scholar and educator

JOE LOUIS
heavyweight champion

RONALD McNAIR
astronaut

MALCOLM X
militant black leader

THURGOOD MARSHALL
Supreme Court justice

ELIJAH MUHAMMAD
religious leader

JESSE OWENS
champion athlete

CHARLIE PARKER
musician

GORDON PARKS
photographer

SIDNEY POITIER
actor

ADAM CLAYTON POWELL, JR.
political leader

LEONTYNE PRICE
opera singer

A. PHILIP RANDOLPH
labor leader

PAUL ROBESON
singer and actor

JACKIE ROBINSON
baseball great

BILL RUSSELL
basketball great

JOHN RUSSWURM
publisher

SOJOURNER TRUTH
antislavery activist

HARRIET TUBMAN
antislavery activist

NAT TURNER
slave revolt leader

DENMARK VESEY
slave revolt leader

MADAM C. J. WALKER
entrepreneur

BOOKER T. WASHINGTON
educator

HAROLD WASHINGTON
politician

WALTER WHITE
civil rights leader and author

RICHARD WRIGHT
author

ON
ACHIEVEMENT

Coretta Scott King

BEFORE YOU BEGIN this book, I hope you will ask yourself what the word excellence means to you. I think that it's a question we should all ask, and keep asking as we grow older and change. Because the truest answer to it should never change. When you think of excellence, perhaps you think of success at work; or of becoming wealthy; or meeting the right person, getting married, and having a good family life.

Those important goals are worth striving for, but there is a better way to look at excellence. As Martin Luther King, Jr., said in one of his last sermons, "I want you to be first in love. I want you to be first in moral excellence. I want you to be first in generosity. If you want to be important, wonderful. If you want to be great, wonderful. But recognize that he who is greatest among you shall be your servant."

My husband, Martin Luther King, Jr., knew that the true meaning of achievement is service. When I met him, in 1952, he was already ordained as a Baptist preacher and was working towards a doctoral degree at Boston University. I was studying at the New England Conservatory and dreamed of accomplishments in music. We married a year later, and after I graduated the following year we moved to Montgomery, Alabama. We didn't know it then, but our notions of achievement were about to undergo a dramatic change.

You may have read or heard about what happened next. What began with the boycott of a local bus line grew into a national movement, and by the time he was assassinated in 1968 my husband had fashioned a black movement powerful enough to shatter forever the practice of racial segregation. What you may not have read about is where he got his method for resisting injustice without compromising his religious beliefs.

He adopted the strategy of nonviolence from a man of a different race, who lived in a distant country, and even practiced a different religion. The man was Mahatma Gandhi, the great leader of India, who devoted his life to serving humanity in the spirit of love and nonviolence. It was in these principles that Martin discovered his method for social reform. More than anything else, those two principles were the key to his achievements.

This book is about black Americans who served society through the excellence of their achievements. It forms a part of the rich history of black men and women in America—a history of stunning accomplishments in every field of human endeavor, from literature and art to science, industry, education, diplomacy, athletics, jurisprudence, even polar exploration.

Not all of the people in this history had the same ideals, but I think you will find something that all of them have in common. Like Martin Luther King, Jr., they all decided to become "drum majors" and serve humanity. In that principle—whether it was expressed in books, inventions, or song—they found something outside themselves to use as a goal and a guide. Something that showed them a way to serve others, instead of living only for themselves.

Reading the stories of these courageous men and women not only helps us discover the principles that we will use to guide our own lives but also teaches us about our black heritage and about America itself. It is crucial for us to know the heroes and heroines of our history and to realize that the price we paid in our struggle for equality in America was dear. But we must also understand that we have gotten as far as we have partly because America's democratic system and ideals made it possible.

We are still struggling with racism and prejudice. But the great men and women in this series are a tribute to the spirit of our democratic ideals and the system in which they have flourished. And that makes their stories special and worth knowing.

RONALD McNAIR

1

"ALL SYSTEMS GO"

O N THE CLEAR but chilly morning of January 28, 1986, thousands of people waited expectantly at the Kennedy Space Center on Florida's Cape Canaveral. They had gathered to witness a 20th-century marvel: the launching of a spacecraft. The space shuttle *Challenger* had been scheduled for lift-off at 9:38 A.M., but officials, concerned about the unseasonably cold weather, had postponed the flight. Now, at about 11:00 A.M., the launch appeared to be imminent.

Among the Space Center's impatient onlookers were friends and relatives of the *Challenger*'s seven-member crew, photographers, television and newspaper reporters, technicians from the National Aeronautics and Space Administration (NASA), and a small army of ordinary citizens, all of them eager to watch an awesome feat of American technology and engineering. Across the nation, millions of other Americans watched the scene on television.

Twenty-four space-shuttle missions, each successful, had preceded this one. Although some of the early hair-trigger tension had eased, the crowd still crackled with excitement. Not everybody in the crowd completely understood the tremendously sophisticated knowledge behind the undertaking, but they all knew another chapter of history was about to unfold.

Ronald McNair, America's second black astronaut, stands by a model of the shuttle Challenger. *An MIT-educated physicist from Lake City, South Carolina, McNair made his first spaceflight in 1984; two years later, he boarded the* Challenger *for his second venture into space.*

Space fans were especially intrigued by this mission because of its unusual, "all-American" crew. Among its five astronauts were one white woman and four men: one black, one Japanese American, and two white. Rounding out the crew were two civilians, a female schoolteacher and a male engineer. For the press, it was a dream team.

The white male astronauts were Francis R. (Dick) Scobee, 46, of Cle Elum, Washington; and Michael J. Smith, 40, of Beaufort, North Carolina. Scobee,

Members of the Challenger's "dream team" gather for a portrait before their January 28, 1986, flight. Seated (from left to right) are pilot Michael Smith, Commander Dick Scobee, and mission specialist McNair. Standing (from left) are mission specialist Ellison Onizuka, payload specialists Christa McAuliffe and Gregory Jarvis, and mission specialist Judith Resnik.

the spacecraft commander, was an engineer and a Vietnam War combat veteran. This would be his second space trip; he had made the first, as a mission pilot, in 1984. Scobee was especially adept at handling large, heavy aircraft. Smith, the pilot on this launch, was a decorated navy test pilot. A space rookie, he was already looking forward to his second flight because, he had joked, he believed this first flight would be so exciting he would probably miss something.

The female astronaut was flight engineer Judith A. Resnik, 36, a doctor of electrical engineering and classical pianist from Akron, Ohio. Intensely dedicated to the space program, Resnik would be a mission specialist on this flight, responsible for operating the shuttle's movable arm. If all went according to plan, the arm would put a $100-million tracking and data relay satellite into orbit, a principal aim of this *Challenger* mission. Resnik was the second American woman in space, and this was her second launch.

The astronaut of Japanese descent was 39-year-old Ellison S. Onizuka, a Hawaiian-born air force lieutenant colonel. Like Resnik, "El" Onizuka was a mission specialist on his second flight. An engineer and a test pilot with 74 hours in space behind him, Onizuka would be responsible for deploying the satellite once the *Challenger* was in orbit.

The flight's civilians were Gregory B. Jarvis, 41, of Detroit, Michigan; and Boston-born Sharon Christa McAuliffe, 37. Jarvis, an electrical engineer and payload specialist on this mission, was a satellite designer for the Hughes Aircraft Company. Bumped off two earlier missions by politicians, Jarvis had been waiting to go into space since 1984. McAuliffe, on the other hand, was not an engineer, not an astronaut or a technician, not part of the U.S. space program. A New Hampshire schoolteacher, she had been selected from more than 11,000 applicants to be the first private American citizen in space. The public seemed to identify with McAuliffe, who had received more press coverage than any of the other participants in this mission.

The *Challenger*'s seventh crew member was 35-year-old Ronald E. McNair of Lake City, South Carolina, a mission specialist on his second spaceflight. McNair's training as a physicist would be vital to a central part of this mission, the deployment of a small recoverable satellite that would observe and photo-

Expecting to board the Challenger within hours, astronaut Ronald McNair and his wife, Cheryl, check the time at the Kennedy Space Center in January 1986. McNair, usually shy about facing reporters and photographers, was all smiles before this trip.

graph Halley's comet. McNair was America's second black astronaut. (The first, Guion Stewart Bluford, Jr., made his initial flight, also aboard the *Challenger*, in 1983.)

Like his colleagues, McNair was growing impatient on this Tuesday morning. He and the other crew members, wearing blue space suits and black boots, had been lying flat on their backs, strapped into their takeoff positions on the *Challenger* since 8:36 A.M. Would this be another no-launch day like the day before? And the day before that? And the day before that? Saturday's launch had been canceled because of the delayed departure of an earlier flight. On Sunday, it had rained at Cape Canaveral. On

Shooting aloft on dazzling columns of orange fire, the Challenger roars into the Florida sky. Mission 51-L, McNair's second spaceflight, was the 25th shuttle trip for the National Aeronautics and Space Administration (NASA); the space agency had launched its first shuttle, the Columbia, on April 12, 1981.

Monday, it had been double trouble: first a sticky bolt on the outside hatch handle, then gusty winds. Another no-go.

The mission crew knew that this time the problem might again be weather. The sky was a crisp blue, but the temperature had dropped to the low 20s during the night. By 8:44 A.M., it had warmed up to 26 degrees Fahrenheit, but the launchpad structure remained festooned with icicles. NASA officials feared that ice, breaking off the structure during lift-off, could damage the sensitive outside skin of the *Challenger*. But as the sun rose, the ice began to melt. NASA officials reached a decision: The launch was on. McNair and his companions relaxed a bit. The countdown continued. All systems go.

At T minus 0:06 (six seconds before lift-off) the *Challenger*'s main engines began to fire. Speaking by radio to the crew, Scobee said, "There they go, guys." McNair glanced at the blue Florida sky outside the spacecraft window. He and the others now felt the ground-shaking, controlled explosion that blasted the *Challenger* off the launchpad in titanic clouds of billowing white smoke. On the ground, observers cheered, screamed, and applauded as the spacecraft ascended on twin columns of yellow-orange fire. Resnik shouted, "Aaall riiight!" The voice of launch control boomed over the Space Center: "Lift-off! Lift-off of the 25th space shuttle mission and it has cleared the tower!"

Like a great silver bullet, the *Challenger* streaked skyward. ✺

2

"GIFTED HE WAS"

Ronald McNair (holding doll), two, and his brother Carl, Jr., three, at their home in Lake City, South Carolina. Ronald, the middle McNair son (brother Eric would arrive in 1956), showed an early aptitude for learning. Reading by the age of three, he caused a local uproar when he invaded the town's whites-only "public" library six years later. "The quality of his uniqueness showed up early," noted his mother.

RONALD ERWIN McNAIR was born in Lake City, South Carolina, on October 21, 1950. He was the second son of Carl and Pearl McNair, whose firstborn, Carl, Jr., had arrived in 1949; the McNairs' third and last son, Eric, would arrive in 1956. Pearl McNair taught school; her husband worked as an automobile mechanic.

In the mid-1950s, Lake City was a fairly typical South Carolina country town. Surrounded by fertile tobacco fields and small farms, it was a quiet place, steeped in the traditional customs and practices of the South—one of which was segregation. All the students in Pearl McNair's school were black. As well as attending a segregated school, they watched Saturday afternoon movies from a segregated balcony and bought their postmovie ice cream from a segregated counter. They sat in separate waiting rooms at bus stations; when they boarded a bus, they sat in the back. And if they wanted a book from Lake City's small library, they could just go on wanting it. The library was reserved for whites. So was the town's only park.

Black adults in the McNairs' hometown may have resented their second-class status, but few raised their voices in complaint. In the midcentury South, blacks who broke the unwritten rules of behavior might find themselves in trouble. Members of such white-supremacist groups as the Ku Klux Klan made it their business to keep blacks "in their place." Hooded night riders still roamed, beating "uppity" blacks, burning crosses in their yards, even lynching them. Whites, too, were subjected to Klan reprisals if they agitated for change in racial matters.

Like his friends, Ronald McNair was unwelcome at the candy stand in Probst's movie theater. After they left the balcony on Saturdays, the black children headed for M & D Drugs, up Main Street and past the railroad tracks that ran through Lake City. Inside the drugstore, white youngsters sipped their sodas at the counter; black children bought their ice cream from the freezer outside and ate it on the street.

Surprisingly, this state of affairs seemed to cause Ronald and his group little distress. Speaking to a reporter years later, McNair's boyhood friend Dozier Witherspoon Montgomery said, "The segregated South did not affect us as deeply as it might have. Though we lived in the Deep South, [Ronald and I] both had a parent who was a teacher. They sheltered their sons and were protective. So we really weren't that conscious of problems."

Pearl McNair and her family were indeed protective; they also expected a great deal of their children. The boys' aunt, Lela M. Austin, taught school and, like Pearl, often talked about the importance of education. Carl McNair, who had never finished high school, deeply regretted his own lack of education and pushed his sons to excel. Ronald McNair was clearly a bright child, but his natural intelligence was undoubtedly sharpened by the education-minded adults who surrounded him in his childhood years.

A robed Georgia family attends an early 1950s rally of the Ku Klux Klan, a white-supremacist organization that used burning crosses and other sinister symbols to terrorize blacks. In McNair's childhood years, most of Lake City's black citizens kept discreetly silent about racial discrimination.

    The McNairs' weather-beaten wooden house on Moore Street overflowed with books, and Ronald learned to read at the age of three. When he and his brothers were older, their parents bought them an encyclopedia—an uncommon sight in any home, black or white, in sleepy little Lake City. "Ours was a studying house," Pearl McNair said years after her boys had grown up.

    Pearl may have taught her son to love books, but it was Carl McNair who arranged an early start for the boy's formal education. Changing the date on Ronald's birth certificate, his father enrolled him in school at the age of four, putting him in the same class with his older brother. Pearl McNair was reportedly not pleased with this deception, but her husband stood firm. "He was more than ready," said Carl McNair later, "and I didn't see any sense in keeping him home."

Ronald turned into a serious reader, devouring the books his family bought and borrowing volumes from friends and neighbors. Still, he longed for more books, wishing he could stand amid the cool aisles of Lake City's whites-only "public" library. Finally, when Ronald was about nine years old, he took action. "He decided to go to the library, and he refused to leave," recalled his mother later.

"The library workers called me," continued Pearl McNair. "I rushed over and found police cars outside the building. Ron was sitting on the charge desk, holding a pile of books in his lap. His little legs hung down, not reaching the floor. I was pleased that he didn't want any trouble, just the books. He wanted to study." Young McNair had changed a small piece of history. "From then on," his mother recalled proudly, "Ron was allowed to borrow books from the library whenever he wished."

From his earliest years, Ronald McNair's teachers recognized him as a serious, studious young man, clearly a cut above the average. As T. R. Cooper, principal of Ronald's elementary school, said later, "The term 'gifted' was not in general use, but gifted he was."

"Ron played," Dozier Montgomery recalled, "but he was always serious. Studies came first." Inseparable friends, Dozier and Ronald were also competitors. "If I got 99 percent [on a test]," Montgomery later told an interviewer, "Ron got 100." The two did their homework together after school and went to the movies together on the weekend. Fondly recalling the magazine rack at the old-fashioned M & D drugstore,

Montgomery said, "We bought comic books there. Ron was also into science fiction. He always liked space books."

Another grade-school friend, Rachel Scott, agreed. "I remember in elementary school when there was all this talk about *Sputnik* [the Soviet satellite launched in 1957]," recalled Scott years later. "That's all Ronald talked about—*Sputnik*, *Sputnik*, *Sputnik*. We got tired of hearing it."

Ronald McNair's childhood, however, was defined by more than schoolwork, movies, and books about space travel. Money was in short supply in the McNair family; teachers, especially black teachers, received very low salaries, and Carl, Sr., as he later told an *Ebony* magazine reporter, never made more than $55 per week in those days. "I taught my sons the auto body trade," McNair told *Ebony*, "and during the summer months they worked sunup to sundown picking cotton and beans, all for just $4 a day."

While her boys were still in elementary school, Pearl McNair decided to go back to school herself. Eager to improve her family's prospects, she drove 600 miles each week, commuting between Lake City and Orangeburg in order to earn her master's degree in education at South Carolina State College.

In the late 1950s, Pearl and Carl McNair faced a difficult task: telling their sons that they had decided to separate. The break at least was not a bitter one. Carl McNair moved to New York City, but he returned to Lake City for summers, holidays, and important family occasions. During the summer months, he coached the town youngsters' baseball team; Ronald played a good second base. "Carl [Sr.] always communicated," Pearl McNair recalled later, "and the boys had time with their dad . . . while I taught summer school."

Nevertheless, Ronald missed his father painfully. Helping to compensate for his absence were Ronald's

McNair's maternal grandparents, Mabel and Jim Montgomery, celebrate Christmas at their daughter Pearl's home. Ronald adored his grandparents and found them a great comfort after his parents split up in the late 1950s. "As a youngster, he helped in his grandfather's business," recalled Pearl McNair. "He helped keep the books. [He] always wanted to be doing something, to help."

grandparents, Mabel and Jim Montgomery. Pearl McNair later recalled that of all her sons, Ronald was the most attached to his grandparents. "As a youngster, he helped in his grandfather's business, which was selling crates," she said. "Besides acting as delivery boy, Ron helped to keep the books." Her middle son, added Pearl McNair, "always wanted to be doing something, to help. He was very helpful in the house. In the kitchen, everywhere. The quality of uniqueness showed up early. We always knew he was a bit different."

Always close to his grandparents, Ronald was to have a special reason to be proud of Mabel Montgomery. One day in the future, he would graduate from college. At the same time, his older brother,

Carl, would receive his college diploma, and his younger brother, Eric, would graduate from high school. Two other McNair relatives would also receive high school diplomas on that red-letter day: one of Aunt Lela Austin's daughters and Grandmother Mabel Montgomery, who earned her diploma at the age of 65.

As Ronald McNair was growing up in Lake City in the 1950s and 1960s, events in the rest of the world were shaping the way Americans live today. In 1950, the year of Ronald McNair's birth, color television was introduced in the United States. In 1954, when McNair was four years old, Dr. Jonas Salk introduced a revolutionary new polio vaccine. Salk's discovery virtually eliminated polio, the crippling, often deadly disease that had stalked generations of young Americans.

In October 1957, the Soviet Union startled the world with its launching of *Sputnik* (Fellow Traveler), the world's first artificial satellite. The 184-pound *Sputnik* made scientific history and set off a round of frantic activity among American physicists. In January 1958, the United States joined the Soviets in space with the successful launch of *Explorer I*, a 31-pound satellite fired from Cape Canaveral.

Two years later, the United States launched the world's first weather satellite, *Tiros 1*. In 1961, the Soviets scored another space coup by sending a man into space. Twenty-seven-year-old Yuri Gagarin circled the globe in 108 minutes. One month later, astronaut Alan B. Shepard, Jr., became the first U.S. spaceman.

By the end of the decade, America had an even greater feat to cheer about: a stunning new chapter in space history. "That's one small step for man, one giant leap for mankind," said U.S. astronaut Neil A. Armstrong, the first human being to set foot on the moon.

Shepard, Armstrong, and the rest of America's space pioneers were white men. At this stage in the nation's history, few opportunities—in science, government, education, or other prestigious fields—existed for blacks. But times were changing. In the mid-1950s, America's long-entrenched racism began to show the first signs of weakening.

Although the Constitution's Fourteenth and Fifteenth Amendments guaranteed "equal justice under law" to all Americans, the policy of "separate but equal"—in schools, transportation, housing, and public facilities—had long ruled the land. In 1954, attorney Thurgood Marshall of the National Association for the Advancement of Colored People (NAACP) brought a series of school cases before the Supreme Court, arguing that separate schools could never be equal. After hearing the black attorney's powerful arguments, the Court ruled segregated schools unconstitutional. The decision would not be fully implemented for years, but it marked the end of government-approved segregation.

Rosa Parks, a black seamstress from Montgomery, Alabama, struck another early blow for black civil liberties. Exhausted after a day's work in 1955, Parks defied local rules by refusing to give up her bus seat to a white man. That courageous act led to a year-long black boycott of Montgomery's buses. The bus strike, organized by a young clergyman named Martin Luther King, Jr., resulted in a U.S. Supreme Court decision that ruled bus segregation unconstitutional.

By the early 1960s, blacks were learning how to obtain their rights. Peaceful marches, lunch-counter sit-ins, black voter-registration drives, and other tactics eventually led to the Civil Rights Act of 1964, which outlawed racial discrimination in voting, employment, education, and public facilities. The Voting Rights Act of 1965 gave the federal government power to enforce integration at the polls, and the

Awed Muscovites contemplate a
model of Sputnik I, the 184-
pound artificial satellite launched
by the Soviet Union in 1957.
Spurred by the Soviets' success,
competitive American scientists
launched their own satellite, Explorer I, three months later.

America's first team of spacemen, the Project Mercury astronauts, proudly model their working apparel in April 1959. In the front row (left to right) are Walter M. Schirra, Jr., Donald K. Slayton, John H. Glenn, Jr., and Scott Carpenter. Standing behind them are (from left) Alan B. Shepard, Jr., Virgil I. ("Gus") Grissom, and L. Gordon Cooper. Until 1978, NASA selected only white males to be astronauts.

Civil Rights Act of 1968 prohibited discrimination
in housing.

Few of these changes had an immediate effect,
especially in the rural South. Pearl McNair continued
to teach in Lake City's segregated schools, and her
sons continued to attend them. But new roads were
being paved, and one day, Ronald McNair would
walk them proudly.

3

MOVING UP

I T WAS THE END of summer, time to get the football team organized. In Lake City, Jack T. Williams, coach of all-black Carver High School, was sizing up the hopefuls. Recalling the scene later, Williams said he thought the candidates did not look "too bad." Then his glance fell on one of the boys, and his spirits fell immediately.

It was not any one thing, said Williams; it was the overall picture. This boy wore glasses over his big dark eyes. He weighed 145 pounds, tops, and measured perhaps five feet eight, no more. And he had a look on his face that said "honor roll," not "sack the quarterback." The coach was not impressed. "This guy," he thought, "is not gonna pan out."

But, Williams recalled happily, he was wrong. That year, number 21 (also known as Ronald McNair) became a starting linebacker for the Carver Panthers. "He was vicious," said Williams admiringly. "Total football player." It was determination, according to the coach. "Anything Ronald set out to do, he did."

McNair, seen here in his college yearbook picture, was known as a perfectionist at Carver High School. "All his teachers knew he would go further than the average child," recalled one Carver instructor.

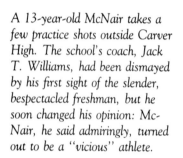

A 13-year-old McNair takes a few practice shots outside Carver High. The school's coach, Jack T. Williams, had been dismayed by his first sight of the slender, bespectacled freshman, but he soon changed his opinion: McNair, he said admiringly, turned out to be a "vicious" athlete.

Although Coach Williams came to admire Ronald McNair, he had trouble telling him apart from his brother Carl, who was also on the team. The coach wound up calling them "the Gismo brothers"—Big Gismo and Little Gismo.

Little Gismo may have been a terror on Carver High's football field, but it was in the classroom that he really excelled. Always serious about getting good grades, he became a perfectionist in high school. If he got less than 100 on a test, he wanted to know why. What had he not understood?

Reminiscing about his classmate many years later, Lake City councilman Wilford Barr said, "We all knew that Ron was smarter than the rest of us. We all knew that he was going to get that 100 on a test. However, his determination made the rest of us eager to study hard to at least get a 99."

Another former McNair classmate, Charles K. Wilson, felt the same way. Both enthusiastic Boy Scouts (McNair reached the level of Star Scout), the two attended camp together one summer. Most of the boys, Wilson recalled later, proved they were "hip" by displaying an Afro comb in their back pocket. Not McNair. "Ron always had a slide rule sticking out of his pocket instead," said Wilson. "During Boy Scout camp, you'd see Ron off to himself reading a book and thumbing his slide rule."

Years after McNair had graduated from high school, Carver economics teacher Harry Fleming talked to an interviewer about his star pupil. "All his teachers knew he would go further than the average child," said Fleming. "He was exceedingly bright, the class leader. His adrenaline never stopped flowing. He was always prodding his teachers to 'go faster,' even when you already thought you were going faster. If you didn't," Fleming added, "Ron, like so many gifted children, became bored."

Fleming also recalled McNair as a very well organized person. "He was always clean and neat and wanted everything to be in its place," said his former teacher. "This sense of organization seemed to extend to all areas of his life."

"Whatever Ronald did, it had to be a challenge," added his old friend Wallace Scott. "If something wasn't a challenge, Ronald just wouldn't bother with it."

Such a young man—studious, well organized, praised by his teachers—might have been a little *too* good, a little hard to take. Not so, declared Dozier Montgomery: "He was all right."

To demonstrate his point, Montgomery described the "great lab case": One day after school, McNair and his friend Archie Alford decided to perform an experiment in the chemistry lab. They filled a sink with water, then threw in a large dose of sodium.

The mixture promptly exploded, filling the room with dense black smoke. Shaken but unhurt, the boys scrambled out of the lab before anyone could place them at the scene of the crime. School officials eventually cracked the case, but they were "pretty lenient" with the culprits, Montgomery recalled. McNair and Alford restricted future chemistry experiments to regular school hours.

McNair's high school record suggests an unusually well rounded young man. He had a girlfriend and got top grades. He was a football player, a baseball star, and a member of the basketball and track teams. He also played an accomplished saxophone in the Carver High School band. "Most people think Ron always played sax," recalled Dozier Montgomery, "but the clarinet was his first love. Whatever, he was good at it." McNair was so good at it, in fact, that for a time he considered making music his career.

McNair, Montgomery, and Alford promised to stay in touch after high school, and they did. Montgomery was to become a math teacher in South Carolina; Alford, still fascinated by chemistry, would teach that subject in Miami. ("The Carver High School class of '67," noted Montgomery, "produced quite a few teachers.") Although they would wind up in different states—McNair was to move to California to work as a physicist—the three remained close friends, getting together whenever they could.

Carver High School was a rambling old building not far from the McNair home. In those days, when integration had yet to take effect in Lake City, Carver remained "separate" but definitely not "equal" to the white high school. Its black students often used books and equipment passed down from the white school, and they often had to supply their own educational materials. When the chemistry teacher had no money to buy hydrochloric acid for lab experiments, for example, students brought in vinegar as an acidic sub-

*Attempting to enter Central High
School in Little Rock, Arkansas,
in 1957, Elizabeth Eckford finds
her way blocked by national
guardsmen. The U.S. Supreme
Court had declared segregation
unconstitutional in 1954, but Little Rock and many other southern
communities defiantly retained
"separate but equal" schools for
years afterward. When McNair
graduated from Lake City's
Carver High in 1967, he had
never attended an integrated class.*

stitute. And when the track team needed a place to practice, team members leveled their own track.

Carver, on the other hand, had something very special of its own: its teaching staff. Backed by determined parents, Carver's teachers demanded the best of their students. Day in and day out, McNair and his classmates heard the same message: If they wanted to get anywhere in life, they would have to be not only as good as but better than the white students. If they got tired of hearing that in the classroom, they could go home and hear it again.

Dozier Montgomery recalled the words of Carver High's principal, P. C. Lemmon: "Never say, 'That'll do.' If you can do that, you can do better." Montgomery added, "It must have stuck with Ronald."

Over and over, Carver's teachers told their students that success started with a college education. The instructors' counsel sank in: About 50 of the 150 students who graduated with McNair—an unusually large proportion for southern blacks in the 1960s—went on to higher education. Like other college-bound southern blacks of the day, they faced limited choices: College usually meant a regional black institution affiliated with the applicant's church.

The McNairs were devout Methodists; Ronald, recalled his mother, had always been church oriented. As a little boy, he sang in the choir of the Wesley United Methodist Church, of which his grandfather was treasurer. In later years, Ronald McNair helped organize and keep track of the church's finances.

"Ron was always concerned with physical activities. He kept his body in shape as well as his mind. And through his church, he also saw after his soul," recalled Pearl McNair. "People often thought it odd that a scientist was into religion and believed in the Lord," she said. "But Ron never missed church if he could help it." Whenever McNair came home to visit his mother, she added, "about the first thing he did was to go to his home church."

To no one's surprise, Ronald McNair was named valedictorian of his graduating class. Most of his college-bound friends who were Methodists planned to attend Claflin, a small South Carolina college that specialized in training teachers. Not inclined toward teaching, McNair applied for—and received—a scholarship from North Carolina Agricultural and Technical State University. His brother Carl was admitted to the same school, a large institution in Greensboro, about 170 miles from Lake City.

Celebrated for its science and engineering programs, North Carolina A&T was founded in 1891. Among its better-known alumni is civil rights and political leader Jesse Jackson, seven years ahead of McNair at A&T. An admirer of his fellow alumnus, Jackson later commented on McNair's participation in the space program. He chose it, said Jackson, because it was the "highest way he could contribute to the system that gave him so much."

McNair entered college as a music major, but his guidance counselor persuaded him to switch to physics. "I think you're good enough," the counselor told him. That was enough for McNair.

But McNair had set himself a difficult course. He soon realized that despite the best intentions of his teachers at Carver, his education had serious gaps; under the "separate but equal" doctrine, the severely underfunded Carver had been unable to supply its students with a competitively broad range of courses. Determined to make up for what he had missed, McNair studied furiously at A&T. He had specialized in working hard in both elementary school and high school, and he was not about to give up now. Ronald McNair never gave up.

During his freshman year, McNair somehow found time to pursue a new activity: karate. He went

Suited up for battle, black-belt holder McNair (left) and a fellow karate student, William Perry, assume a challenging posture for their college yearbook photographer. By his senior year at North Carolina A&T, McNair had acquired a fifth-degree black belt and qualification as a karate instructor.

at it with the same diligence he applied to everything he did. Starting out with 200 students, the arduous karate class was down to 5 by the end of the semester. Two years later, the class had dwindled to just one student—Ronald McNair. Before he finished, McNair was to acquire a fifth-degree black belt, symbol of karate's highest rank, and to demonstrate impressive skills as an instructor.

By the time McNair reached the midpoint of his undergraduate studies at A&T, his future was firmly committed to science. In his junior year, he became part of a new North-South educational exchange program. Under this plan, promising black college students spent a year at the Massachusetts Institute of Technology (MIT) in Cambridge, Massachusetts; in return, MIT sent professors to teach at black colleges in the South.

In the fall of 1969, McNair headed for Cambridge. He was about to discover a new—and not always friendly—world. ◖◗

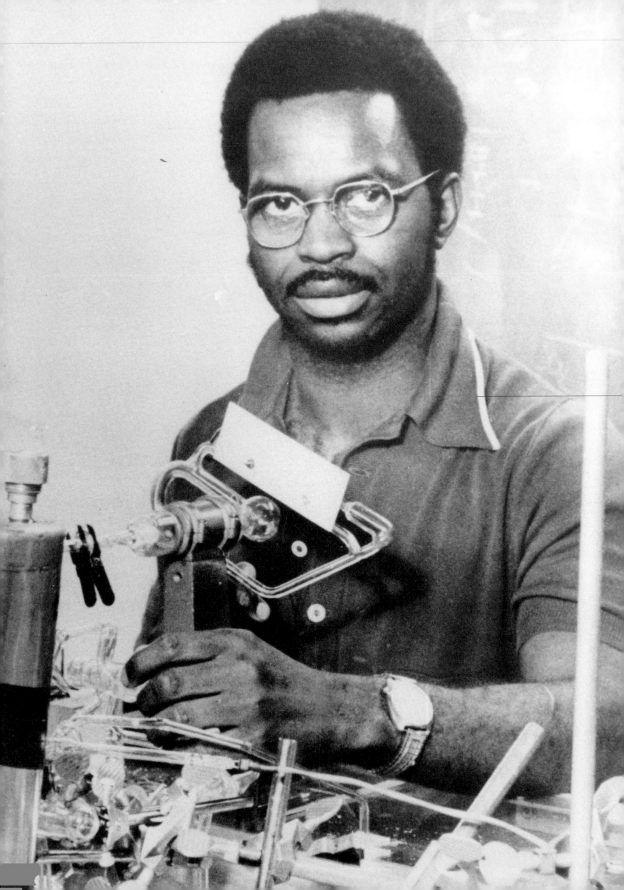

4

"I HAD TO COMPETE WITH THE BEST"

McNair, who spent his junior year at the Massachusetts Institute of Technology (MIT), performs an experiment in the school's Spectroscopy Laboratory. Discovering that his southern, largely segregated education had not prepared him for the northern institution's tough standards, McNair worked harder than ever.

IN 1962, ONLY SEVEN YEARS before McNair entered MIT, another young black man had made national headlines simply by entering college. James Meredith's effort to attend the all-white University of Mississippi marked the start of a long and bitter struggle that polarized the nation but eventually resulted in the affirmation of all Americans' civil rights.

The University of Mississippi, founded in 1844, had never admitted a black student. Meredith, an academically qualified war veteran, obtained a federal court order authorizing his admittance. Yet Mississippi governor Ross Barnett flatly refused to let him enroll. Protected by federal marshals, Meredith tried to enter "Ole Miss" four times; four times he was turned away.

Meredith's fifth effort succeeded, but it sparked a riot that killed 2 people, injured 375 others, and ended only after 3,000 federal troops enforced order.

One year later, shortly before McNair's 13th birthday, nearly a quarter of a million people demonstrated their support for civil rights with a spectacular march on Washington, D.C. The vast crowd of blacks and whites listened, as did the rest of the nation, to a black leader explaining his dream of justice. "There will be neither rest nor tranquillity in America," said the Reverend Martin Luther King, Jr., "until the Negro is granted his citizenship rights. . . . No, we are not satisfied and we will not be satisfied until justice rolls down like water and righteousness like a mighty stream."

In 1965, King led a march from Selma, Alabama, to the state capital, Montgomery, to protest restrictions on black voting rights. A few hours after the 25,000 marchers arrived in Montgomery, Ku Klux Klan members shot and killed a white civil rights worker at the wheel of her car. In 1968, the year of McNair's 18th birthday, King himself was shot to death as he stood on the balcony of a motel in Memphis, Tennessee.

News of these historic and tragic events swirled around Lake City during McNair's most formative years. And yet, as Dozier Montgomery later recalled, the nation's tumultuous civil rights battles seemed far away to the young people in that small southern community. At home, no one talked much about prejudice or segregation.

Accompanied by federal marshals, James Meredith (center) approaches a classroom at the University of Mississippi in 1962. The black veteran's effort to enroll at the all-white school triggered an uproar, but after five tries and a riot that took two lives, he finally succeeded. With two years of college credits already earned, Meredith peacefully graduated from the university in 1963.

America was gradually moving toward racial justice, but in 1969, when Ronald McNair first went north to Massachusetts, that goal had not yet become a reality.

MIT, situated on the banks of the Charles River in Cambridge, had been founded in 1861. Its reputation in the field of science was guaranteed to daunt even the most self-confident student. As McNair later joked, "Even the janitors at MIT had master's degrees."

White students who entered MIT at the time could expect an excellent education. They could also

The "Spirit of '65"—four civil rights demonstrators echoing the celebrated revolutionary war painting "Spirit of '76"—heads for Montgomery, Alabama, in 1965. Along with some 25,000 others, the quartet had joined the Reverend Martin Luther King, Jr.'s March for Freedom, a multiracial protest against the South's antiblack voting laws.

expect to be part of a cultured, gracious center of learning. For their black counterparts, however, this was not always the case in 1969.

McNair had been recruited by MIT under a program aimed at bringing more blacks into the fields of science and engineering. When he enrolled in the institution as a junior, no more than 200 of its 7,500 students were black. Despite the small number of blacks, some of the white students resented them, claiming they were sometimes less qualified than white applicants who had been rejected. And resentment of blacks was not confined to the MIT campus: Working-class Boston whites, strenuously fighting desegregation in their neighborhood schools, often exhibited noisy—and frightening—hostility toward dark-skinned people.

Arriving in the Boston area, McNair probably expected to enjoy such pleasures as listening to the Boston Symphony, strolling the banks of the Charles, and exploring the old city of Boston. What he found were neighborhoods where he dared not walk, and what he heard were the unaccustomed sounds of racial taunts.

But McNair settled down to work as usual, doing his best to ignore racial hostility. After two stimulating semesters in MIT's physics department, he returned to A&T for his senior year. And after that? For a career in physics, a doctorate from MIT would be ideal. But, McNair asked himself, was he ready to return to a school where "even the janitors had master's degrees" and to a city where he had not felt entirely comfortable? "At first I wasn't going," McNair admitted later, "but then I couldn't run away from a challenge. I had to compete with the best." He applied, and MIT accepted him.

MIT was not only one of the nation's finest technical institutions; it was also one of America's most costly. To pay his tuition and living expenses over the next five years, McNair would need financial aid. His college adviser, Tom Sandin, suggested that he try for a fellowship from the Ford Foundation, which often aided black students who demonstrated intellectual abilities and leadership potential. "If you can't give this [fellowship] to Ron McNair," Sandin wrote in his recommendation, "you can't give it to anyone." The Ford Foundation agreed: McNair received his fellowship.

In 1971, he graduated *magna cum laude* (Latin for "with great distinction") from North Carolina Agricultural and Technical State University. Holding a bachelor's degree in physics, he was ready to head north again and to tackle one of the most prestigious—and toughest—graduate schools in America.

Although McNair was prepared for bigotry this time, it was no easier to take. On his way out of a

Three generations celebrate a shower of diplomas in June 1971. On this happy day in McNair family history, Ronald (left) and his brother Carl, Jr. (second from left), received bachelor of science degrees from North Carolina A&T. The 3 high school graduates are the McNairs' cousin; their brother, Eric; and their grandmother, 65-year-old Mabel Montgomery.

karate class in Harvard Square one day, he found himself surrounded by a gang of jeering whites, one of whom jumped him. He got the better of his attacker and escaped, but the taunts rang in his ears. Another time, when he was going to visit a friend in a white neighborhood, a stranger set his dog on him. Again, McNair managed to get away, but memories of this incident, like the other, bothered him for weeks.

Racial animosity was not McNair's only concern. He had been at the top of his class in both high school and college, but in MIT's graduate program he became painfully aware of certain educational lacks. Many of his classmates, products of such top-ranked undergraduate schools as Stanford or Harvard, were far better prepared for MIT than he was. Once again, he was paying the price of his nation's "separate but equal" doctrine.

But Ronald McNair was still the same man, still equipped with the same intelligence and persistence he had always demonstrated. Gritting his teeth, he made up his mind: He would *make it* at MIT. As Michael Feld, director of MIT's Spectroscopy Laboratory and McNair's adviser, put it later, "Given [McNair's] fairly inadequate background, it took tremendous determination to bring himself up to speed, but he was able to muster that kind of resolve."

To catch up with his fellow students, McNair took courses in electrical engineering, advanced physics, and even some undergraduate courses. The white students tended to study in groups, but McNair did most of his studying alone in one of MIT's basement laboratories.

Recalling his own days as a minority student at MIT, McNair's classmate Gregory C. Chisholm later said, "We all recognized the tenuousness [uncertainty] of our positions in the country, in the city, and at the Institute. Holding on and securing ourselves [at MIT] was no mean task." Chisholm said that some black students rebelled and some denied there was a problem, but "others looked to the future, like Ron McNair, who made a downpayment with his commitment to excellence."

Little by little, McNair's hard work and determination paid off. His progress was steady. He was making it—although not without some setbacks. To qualify for a doctorate, physics students had to pass a five-hour qualifying examination. The first time McNair took the test, he failed it. Disappointed but not discouraged, McNair went back to his books, took the test again, and passed it with flying colors. Then he ran into another, even worse, problem: He lost the notebook in which he had recorded all the data from his experiments.

"That was two years' worth of work," noted adviser Michael Feld. "But Ronald never complained. He went back to work in the laboratory, and in a few months' time the second set of data was complete, and it turned out better than the first data. This was typical of the way he worked to accomplish goals." McNair, added Feld, then wrote a "very solid" doctoral thesis on laser physics, followed by several impressive technical publications.

At MIT, McNair helped develop some of the first chemical and high-pressure carbon dioxide lasers. After he graduated, he published a number of papers on lasers and addressed many scientific groups on the subject. His laser studies would also be important in his career as an astronaut.

Utterly intense about his work, McNair still managed to find a little time for fun. He continued to play his saxophone and to practice karate, which he was now qualified to instruct. One evening, after teaching a class at the St. Paul African Methodist Episcopal Church in Cambridge, he attended a pot-luck supper at the church. Also present was a pretty

Graduate students, most of them white, attend an MIT lecture in the mid-1970s. At the start of his years at the Massachusetts institution, McNair felt socially excluded and tense about racial hostility, but he eventually acquired a wide circle of friends, both black and white.

and shy young teacher from Jamaica, New York. Her name was Cheryl Moore, and Ronald McNair fell in love with her almost at once. The instant attraction proved mutual; a short time later, McNair asked Moore to marry him, and she said yes. On June 27, 1976, soon after McNair's graduation from MIT, he and Moore were married at St. Paul's.

Dr. Ronald McNair, 5 feet 8 inches tall, weighing 160 pounds, was now almost 26 years old. It was time for all those years of study and hard work to pay off. And they did. McNair won a plum job as staff physicist at Hughes Research Laboratories in Malibu, California. The McNairs headed west.

At Hughes, one of the world's major centers of advanced laser research, McNair's work included research on lasers for satellite-to-satellite space communications. Unaware of it at the time, he was actually in training for mission-specialist duties aboard the *Challenger*.

One day in 1977, not long after he had started working at Hughes, McNair received a brochure in the mail. It was from NASA. The brochure was to change his life. ✿

5

FROM SPUTNIK
TO THE SHUTTLE

ON JULY 20, 1969, eight years before McNair opened his message from NASA, the agency was tensely awaiting a message of its own. Gathered at NASA's Manned Spacecraft Center in Houston, Texas, technicians and scientists sat in charged silence, hoping for a report that would change scientific history forever. At last, at 4:17 P.M., eastern daylight time, it arrived: Across 245,000 miles of space, the voice of astronaut Neil Armstrong said, "Houston, Tranquillity base here. The *Eagle* has landed."

Armstrong's words marked the greatest triumph in the short history of NASA. Armstrong and his fellow astronaut Edwin Aldrin had just landed their lunar module, *Eagle*, on the moon.

This electrifying moment was the outcome of centuries of dreams. The first person to write about space travel may have been Greek author Lucian of Samosata. In the year A.D. 160, Lucian wrote *True Story*, a tale about a sailing ship blown to the moon in a storm. And the first would-be space traveler was probably Wan Hu, a Chinese scholar who tried to reach the moon in the year 1500. Wan Hu attached

Astronaut Edwin Aldrin inspects the moon's first human footprints, made by his fellow space traveler Neil Armstrong on July 20, 1969. As Armstrong's size 9¼ boot emerged from the lunar module Eagle, *500 million people around the world watched on television, listening in awe as the astronaut spoke the now famous words: "That's one small step for man, one giant leap for mankind."*

47 skyrockets to a chair, strapped himself into it, and holding a kite in each hand, ordered a servant to light the rockets. Unfortunately, both chair and scholar disappeared in a cloud of flame.

In 1678, a British mathematician took a more practical approach. In *Philosophiae Naturalis Principia Mathematica*, one of the greatest intellectual achievements in human history, Sir Isaac Newton actually explained the principles of rocket propulsion. Newton even realized that if an object could be shot from earth with enough speed, it would go into orbit instead of falling back to earth.

Almost 200 years after Newton's revolutionary work, French author Jules Verne wrote *From the Earth to the Moon*, one of the first science-fiction novels. Verne's book convinced thousands of people that spaceflight was a real possibility. Forty-seven years after that, in 1912, American physicist Robert H. Goddard began to experiment with liquid-fueled rockets. Goddard, known as the father of American rocketry, patented a step rocket, one that fired in stages, just as modern rockets do.

The 20th-century space age began in earnest when the Soviet Union launched its first satellite, *Sputnik I*, on October 4, 1957. Americans were shocked. How could the Soviets be so far ahead of the technology-oriented United States? U.S. officials rushed to reassure the public that the Soviets' superiority was only temporary; America's first space effort, however, ended in failure. A Vanguard rocket, scheduled to put a small satellite into orbit in December 1957, exploded on the launchpad.

But after that unlucky beginning, things began to look up for the United States. America launched its first successful satellite, *Explorer I*, on January 31, 1958. A Vanguard firing the following March also turned out to be right on the money. And in that year, NASA was founded to guide America's space programs.

Physicist Robert H. Goddard— one of the first scientists to assert that space could be conquered through the use of rocket propulsion—prepares to demonstrate a new rocket frame in May 1926. NASA officials have acknowledged that without Goddard's pioneering work, it would be "virtually impossible to construct a rocket or launch a satellite."

The U.S.-Soviet "space race" was on. In April 1959, NASA selected seven astronauts for Project Mercury, the first American man-in-space effort. Among the seven were Alan Shepard and John Glenn. On May 5, 1961, Shepard would become the first American in space; Glenn was to be the first American shot into orbit (in February 1962). These "firsts," however, were once again overshadowed by

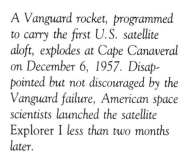

A Vanguard rocket, programmed to carry the first U.S. satellite aloft, explodes at Cape Canaveral on December 6, 1957. Disappointed but not discouraged by the Vanguard failure, American space scientists launched the satellite Explorer I less than two months later.

the Soviets, who put the world's first man into orbit on April 12, 1961.

Cosmonaut Yuri Gagarin's success on the spaceship *Vostok I*—and the ensuing publicity as well as worldwide admiration for the Russians—goaded competitive Americans into action. Soon after the flight, President John F. Kennedy announced the biggest scientific project in American history: the Apollo moon program. Eight years later, on July 20, 1969, a fascinated world, through the magic of television, watched the biggest U.S. "first" of all: American astronaut Neil Armstrong stepped from his spacecraft and walked on the moon.

In 1973, after five more moon landings, NASA began a new project: Skylab, which placed a flying laboratory in orbit around the earth at an altitude of 270 miles. It was Skylab's mission to study the sun, conduct gravity-free experiments, and observe the long-term effects of weightlessness on the human body and mind. Skylab's crews proved that people could work, sleep, and eat high above the earth's protective atmosphere without suffering any permanent ill effects.

For some time, even before the Apollo project began, NASA officials realized they could not continue to send one-way craft into space. It was simply too expensive. In January 1972, NASA announced its readiness to begin development of a "national space transportation system," or space shuttle. A reusable vehicle, the shuttle would be capable of making round trips from earth to space again and again. Its supporters pointed out that the shuttle would be useful for military and commercial purposes as well as for scientific advancement.

"NASA engineers," observed astronaut-author Michael Collins in his 1988 book, *Liftoff*, "were intrigued by the idea of flying one vehicle over and over. It implied a technological maturity, a feeling that space was here to stay. . . . For an aeronautical engineer, the path to reusability was glorious."

The shuttle, as Collins described it, would be "a mature workhorse that would launch vertically, like its rocket predecessors, but fly back to a horizontal landing like a conventional airplane." In fact, the shuttle looks more like a jetliner than a space capsule. It can carry heavy loads into orbit—space-station components, for example—and bring heavy loads back to earth. It can deploy satellites in space, repair them if they malfunction, or return them to earth for overhauling.

The shuttle, a unique and complex space machine, is actually made up of three basic parts: the delta-winged orbiter, the external fuel tank, and the solid rocket boosters.

A beaming Yuri Gagarin appears in First Voyage to the Stars, a Soviet film celebrating the young cosmonaut's historic 1961 space ride. The Soviet Union's success in sending a human into orbit helped spark America's Apollo program, which would put U.S. astronauts on the moon in 1969.

The orbiter—so called, of course, because it orbits the earth—is the "airplane" part, about the size of a DC-9 commercial jet. The front end of the orbiter (the forward fuselage) contains the two-level flight deck, where the crew operates the thousands of switches, dials, and controls needed to operate the craft; the crew's living quarters; and the laboratory area, where mission specialists perform their experiments.

Behind the forward fuselage is the midfuselage, the biggest section of the orbiter. Its huge cargo bay carries the equipment for each mission. Because the cargo area is not pressurized, astronauts must wear their space suits when they enter it. The midfuselage also holds the 50-foot-long Remote Manipulator System (RMS). A robotic arm controlled from the flight deck, the RMS grapples objects in and out of the bay and puts them in orbit. The tail of the orbiter (the aft fuselage) contains the shuttle's five powerful rocket motors.

During lift-off, the orbiter rides piggyback on the external fuel tank, the only part of the space shuttle that is not reused. The tank, 27 feet in diameter, carries 1.5 million pounds of hydrogen and oxygen in separate compartments. Its fuel expended shortly before the shuttle reaches orbit, the tank separates from the orbiter and disintegrates as it reenters the earth's atmosphere. Its remnants are programmed to drop into the ocean.

On each side of the external fuel tank are the slender solid rocket boosters, each as tall as a 15-story building. Each booster contains more than 1 million gallons of a rubbery fuel known as PBAN, stored in a combustion chamber made of 4 steel panels sealed by rubber O-rings. The boosters aid the main engines during the first two minutes and eight seconds of a flight, giving the shuttle enough thrust to escape earth's gravitational pull. When the shuttle reaches an altitude of about 24 miles, the boosters detach. Braked by parachutes, they fall to the ocean, where they are recovered and made ready for reuse.

By early 1981, NASA had completed four space shuttles, each ready to fly to orbit: the *Columbia*, the *Challenger*, the *Discovery*, and the *Atlantis*. The *Columbia* made the first successful shuttle flight on April 12, 1981. *Challenger*'s first mission took place two years later, on April 4. Lighter and stronger than the first shuttle, *Challenger* carried a four-astronaut crew on its maiden voyage.

Challenger became the fleet's star performer, completing nine successful missions by late 1985, when all four orbiters were operational. *Challenger*'s tenth mission was scheduled for January 1986. ❧

6

SPACE TRAINING

RONALD McNAIR'S JOB at Hughes Research Laboratories gave him the chance to use the training and skills he had worked so hard to master. He liked the work and he liked California. So did Cheryl McNair. But in 1976, when McNair received a brochure from NASA, his eyes lit up. The space agency, said the booklet, was looking for qualified scientists to train as mission specialists. McNair turned to his wife. "What do you think," he asked, "about my becoming an astronaut?"

Cheryl McNair thought for a moment, then said, "You have the credentials . . . so try it."

Carl McNair was a bit more skeptical. When Ronald told his brother he was thinking about becoming an astronaut, Carl smiled. "Sure," he said, "and I'm going to be the pope." Atlanta businessman McNair was obviously joking; physicist McNair had never been more serious.

McNair was 1 of about 8,000 people to receive the NASA brochure. Characteristically ignoring his potential competition, he filled out an application for the space program. He was, reported his mother later, "calm and confident" that he would be chosen.

Attired in their new extravehicular mobility units, America's first black astronauts meet the press in January 1978. Mission specialist Guion Stewart Bluford, Jr. (seated), would make his maiden spaceflight in August 1983, mission specialist McNair (left) in February 1984, and pilot Frederick D. Gregory in April 1985.

And he was. In January 1978, a NASA official called with the news: McNair, along with 34 others, had been accepted from a pool of 10,000 prospects as an astronaut candidate. Once again, Ronald and Cheryl McNair packed their bags, this time heading for the Johnson Space Center in Houston, Texas.

McNair knew he was fully qualified to become an astronaut, but he also knew that his selection owed something to politics; NASA officials were anxious to open the space program to minority candidates. As one of the few blacks in the program, McNair found himself the object of more public attention than he wanted. As usual, he focused on his work, ignoring the spotlight. Another black astronaut, McNair's friend Charles F. Bolden, Jr., said later, "I don't think Ron ever thought about it."

In the Houston training program, McNair joined two other blacks, Frederick D. Gregory and Guion Stewart Bluford, both of them colonels in the U.S. Air Force. Gregory, a graduate of the Air Force Academy, had served as a test pilot; Bluford, trained as an aerospace engineer, had flown 65 combat missions in Vietnam, earning the Vietnam Cross of Gallantry with Palm, along with a dozen other decorations.

Like McNair, Bluford was a quiet man, uneasy in the public eye. He did open up enough, however, to tell one reporter what he thought about the astronaut training program. "The job is so fantastic, you don't need a hobby," said Bluford. "The hobby is going to work."

McNair managed to say almost nothing in public about his feelings. Yet he never complained when reporters singled him out for questions. Not surprisingly, McNair's colleagues later remembered him as "the most quiet person in class."

As well as Gregory and Bluford, McNair's Houston classmates included Judy Resnik, Ellison Onizuka, Dick Scobee, and Sally Ride, who would become America's first woman in space. Twelve months after he entered the program, McNair became eligible for the spot of mission specialist, part of the crew in future shuttle flights.

All the astronaut candidates were in excellent physical shape, and most entered the program with impressive credentials either as pilots or as scientists. Nevertheless, all had much to learn. They embarked on a heavy schedule of classes, studying such science and technology courses as advanced mathematics, earth resources, meteorology, guidance and navigation, astronomy, and computer science.

The candidates also had to learn how to live and work in the weightless environment of outer space, where the words *up* and *down* are meaningless. As one veteran astronaut put it, "You carry with you your own body-oriented world . . . in which up is over your head, down is below your feet . . . and you take this world around with you wherever you go."

The candidates trained for functioning in zero gravity with various devices. Among them was the KC-135 jet aircraft, modified for astronaut training; flying in this vehicle gives the effect of riding in a rapidly descending elevator. In the KC-135, McNair and his classmates practiced the techniques of using different pieces of equipment under zero-gravity conditions. They underwent longer periods of weightlessness in a specially designed water tank large enough to hold full-scale mock-ups of spacecraft components and equipment.

Before they go to sleep, astronauts must strap themselves down to keep from floating away; most, however, report that weightlessness is very comfortable for sleeping. The body encounters no pressure points except for the light, reassuring touch of the sleeping bag. Astronauts must even relearn such simple tasks as eating; a too swift movement with a fork or spoon may send food floating away from the diner.

Fledgling astronauts McNair and Rhea Seddon listen to a NASA instructor during a 1979 training exercise in a KC-135 jet aircraft. Specially modified for astronaut training, the KC-135 provides its passengers with the zero-gravity environment they will experience in space.

Weightlessness poses problems for the human body. Many astronauts feel at least slightly nauseous during their first day or two in flight; doctors advise them to move slowly and avoid sudden head movements. Medical specialists have not yet discovered the reason for space nausea, but many compare it to old-fashioned motion sickness. This ailment results when the brain receives different signals from the eye and the inner ear; the ear detects motion, but the eye sees its immediate surroundings as steady, resulting in a feeling of queasiness.

On earth, gravity keeps the body in reasonably good shape, even without exercise; the heart must work constantly in order to pump blood from the feet to the head. With no gravity to work against, the heart becomes lazy. To maintain health, astronauts must exercise all their muscles, including the heart.

When they work outside the shuttle, astronauts need protection against the lack of oxygen in space, against extremes of hot and cold temperatures, and against tiny particles traveling at very high speeds. Outside the shuttle, only the space suit comes between the astronaut and instant death.

Under the space suit, the astronaut wears a one-piece zippered bodysuit. Resembling traditional long underwear, this article is known as the LCVG (liquid cooling and ventilation garment). A network of tubes, carrying cooling water to all parts of the body, is woven into the LCVG. Attached to the astronaut's groin is a urine-collection bag; attached to his or her torso is a container for drinking water.

The astronaut also wears a snugly fitted hat equipped with headphones and a microphone. If any part of the suit should fail, the astronaut would hear a warning signal through the headphones.

A two-piece space suit fits over the LCVG. The wearer dons the bottom section first, then slides head-first into the top part. Joining the two pieces at the waist is a circular metal ring that ensures an airtight fit. Metal rings also attach helmet and gloves. Oxygen enters the suit through the helmet; oxygen, water vapor, and carbon dioxide are removed through ports at the wrists and feet.

Completing the outfit are an oxygen backpack and a reserve pack. An astronaut can work outside the shuttle for about seven hours on the main pack; the reserve pack carries about half an hour of oxygen. Shuttle space suits—in effect tiny, self-contained spacecraft—are built to last for years of wear. Because the astronaut candidates had to become accustomed to working in these pressurized suits, they wore them for many of their training sessions.

"A space flight begins when the technician snaps your helmet down into your neck ring and locks it in place," noted Michael Collins in *Liftoff*. "From that moment on, no outside air will be breathed, only bottled oxygen; no human voice heard, unless electronically piped in through the barrier of the pressure suit. The world can still be seen, but that is all—not smelled, or heard, or felt, or tasted."

The proper use of space suits was, of course, only one of the countless skills an apprentice astronaut had to master. Ronald McNair spent six years in Houston preparing for his first spaceflight. He was living a new kind of life, faced with new challenges. Not all the astronaut candidates could adjust to the demands of training; some "washed out" after the first year.

McNair seemed to manage easily. Charles Bolden, who was a participant in the astronaut training class selected in 1980, called McNair "an exceptional individual." In an interview with *Ebony* magazine, Bolden said, "I don't think any one person could have kept up with Ron to know all the things that he was into. He was absolutely phenomenal. I know he slept, but I'm not sure when. He never had a normal time

that was day or night. Ron did things until they were finished, and if that meant going past midnight, then he did."

Meanwhile, in 1982, the McNairs welcomed the arrival of their first child, Reginald; two years later, the family moved into a comfortable suburban home with a big backyard. Shortly after the move, Cheryl McNair gave birth to a daughter, Joy.

And Ronald McNair continued his training, which sometimes must have seemed endless. He spent many hours in jet aircraft, many hours testing the effects of weightlessness, many hours learning to handle familiar tools that suddenly seemed awkward, many hours adjusting to living in very close quarters with his colleagues.

Astronaut candidate McNair (second row, right) attends a 1978 survival-school class at Vance Air Force Base in Oklahoma. Also listening to the lecture are Ellison Onizuka (second row, left) and Judith Resnik (last row, left), mission specialists who would fly with McNair on the shuttle Challenger.

McNair polishes his skills aboard a spacecraft simulator in mid-1982. Astronaut candidates, who spend hundreds of hours in the extremely realistic simulators, often feel like experienced space travelers by the time they first blast off into space.

As the time approached for McNair's space "debut," the tempo of his training picked up. In order to learn the individual tasks required to fly a spacecraft and then to put them all together in the sequence that would be followed during the actual mission, McNair and his associates started working with space-craft simulators.

These devices provide extremely realistic working conditions. Real spacecraft interiors are duplicated; such instruments as guidance and navigation display are programmed to give the same readings they would

Cheryl and Ronald McNair show off their two-year-old son, Reginald, at the Johnson Space Center in 1984. Soon after they sat for this portrait, the McNairs became the proud parents of their second child, Joy Cheray, born on July 20.

give in flight. And, as one NASA brochure proudly points out, "even out-the-window views of the earth, stars, payloads, and the landing runway are projected onto screens where the spacecraft windows would be." The simulated conditions, says NASA, "are so accurate that most astronauts come back from a mission feeling they had made the same flight many times before."

Astronaut training is methodical, scientific, and deadly serious. It is designed to make missions successful and to keep their participants alive. But finally, for the man or woman who perseveres, who makes the grade, who learns the lessons and overcomes the stress, the big day arrives: the first ride into space. ✤

7

AIMING HIGH

The crew of Mission 41-B prepares to board the Challenger on February 3, 1984. Following Commander Vance Brand are (from left) mission specialists Bruce McCandless II, Robert L. Stewart, and McNair; at rear is pilot Robert L. Gibson. Although the flight ran into some trouble, it produced a number of notable firsts, including a space walk by McCandless and Stewart.

O N FEBRUARY 3, 1984, the moment Ronald McNair had been waiting for arrived at last: Aboard the shuttle *Challenger*, he and five astronaut colleagues blasted off from the Kennedy Space Center at 8:00 A.M.

The *Challenger* was under the command of 52-year-old space veteran Vance Brand, a former test pilot who had commanded the *Columbia* on a November 1982 flight. The other crew members—pilot Robert L. Gibson, 37; and mission specialists Robert L. Stewart, 41; Bruce McCandless II, 46; and Ronald E. McNair, 33—were space rookies.

Mission 41-B had several objectives: to put two satellites into orbit, to test two significant pieces of new equipment, and to perform a number of experiments. The mission accomplished some of its goals, but it also encountered its share of bad luck.

Eight hours into the flight, on time and on target, the *Challenger* crew deployed *Westar 6*, a Western Union communications satellite. To place a satellite in orbit, a mission specialist sets it spinning on a turntable in the shuttle's cargo bay. On release, the

The Challenger, carrying McNair on his first trip into space, roars aloft in a billowing cloud of smoke. Powering the lift-off is a giant external fuel tank and two solid rocket boosters, all to be jettisoned when the orbiter reaches the proper speed and altitude. The external tank is programmed to disintegrate, but the boosters will be parachuted to earth, recovered, and refitted for later flights.

satellite floats away from the orbiter; a rocket motor then fires, boosting it into orbit. On Mission 41-B, however, the rocket's upper-stage motor malfunctioned, and the satellite failed to reach its proper orbit. On day four of the flight, the crew deployed the second satellite, *Palapa B-2*, for the nation of Indonesia. Unfortunately, this satellite, too, fell victim to a faulty rocket motor.

On day five, Stewart and McCandless became the first humans to fly "free" in space. They tested the new Manned Maneuvering Units, jet-propelled backpacks that enabled them to spend a total of 12 hours "space walking" outside the shuttle.

McNair was in charge of operating the shuttle's new 50-foot Remote Manipulator Arm, which would be used on future repair missions. If a deployed satellite is damaged or has failed to achieve its assigned orbit, a shuttle pilot can maneuver his craft close to the satellite. Then, using the mechanical arm, a mission specialist can grab the damaged satellite and haul it into the shuttle's cargo bay for repair or return to earth. (Nine months after Mission 41-B, *Discovery* astronauts would accomplish just such a rescue. Locating the *Westar 6* and the *Palapa B-2*, they grabbed the errant satellites with the shuttle's arm, tucked them into the bay, and brought them back to earth. Both were refitted for later use.)

On day six, McNair conducted a series of experiments on the shuttle's middeck. His subjects included solar cells, pneumatic conveyers, a spectrometer that analyzed gases in and around the orbiter, and a remote sensing camera that recorded images of the earth overflown by the *Challenger*.

NASA managers had decided that when the *Challenger* completed its mission on February 12, it would land at the Kennedy Space Center. This was a first. Each of the previous nine shuttle flights had come in at Edwards Air Force Base, a dry lake in California's

Astronaut Bruce McCandless II walks in space on February 7, 1984. Previous astronauts had ventured outside their orbiters, but McCandless was the first to employ the Manned Maneuvering Unit, a jet-propelled device that allowed him to leave the ship untethered.

Mojave Desert. Edwards's runway is 20 miles long and 7 miles wide; the runway at Cape Canaveral is less than 3 miles long and only 300 feet wide, making landings much more complex.

Another problem presented by a Florida landing is weather. At Edwards, the early-morning weather is usually clear and calm; at the cape, the weather is unpredictable, and a rain squall or fog bank can roll in off the coast without warning.

A landing at Kennedy, however, would save time. When a shuttle comes down in California, it must be loaded onto the top of a giant 747 jet and flown, piggyback, to the launchpad at Kennedy. Because the *Challenger* was scheduled for another launch in April, saving the seven-day turnaround time was important.

The shuttle lands as though it were a glider. Still, observed Michael Collins in *Liftoff*, "The orbiter's final descent would scare the socks off the average glider pilot. It comes screaming down at over 300 mph, at an angle of 20 degrees. . . . At the last moment the pilot drops the [landing] gear and the orbiter touches down at over 200 mph. If the pilot makes a mistake and undershoots or overshoots, that's tough, he crashes, because at this point the orbiter is without engine power and cannot make a second try."

Although Brand had been through 3,000 practice landings and 1 actual landing in the *Columbia*, he was tense about bringing the *Challenger* into the cape. Later, talking to Collins about the landing, he said, "When I got over central Florida, between St. Petersburg and Orlando, I wondered how I was going to get down in time. I had a feeling of great height and speed. Then I went into that spiral staircase."

Brand's comparison of his landing path to a staircase was apt, noted Collins. "The orbiter glides like a stone during its final turn," he explained, "and from [an altitude of] 90,000 feet, [Brand] was on the runway within 6 minutes." At 7:15 A.M., after almost

eight days in space, the *Challenger* was safely back on earth.

When the spacecraft coasted to a stop, McNair and his colleagues tried to get up out of their seats—and found they could not. After more than 191 hours in space, the astronauts needed about 30 minutes to "shake out [their] legs," as one of them put it, before scrambling down the *Challenger*'s ladder to solid ground. Along with former rookies Stewart, McCandless, and Gibson, Ronald McNair was now a full-fledged, seasoned astronaut, with 27 revolutions around the earth behind him.

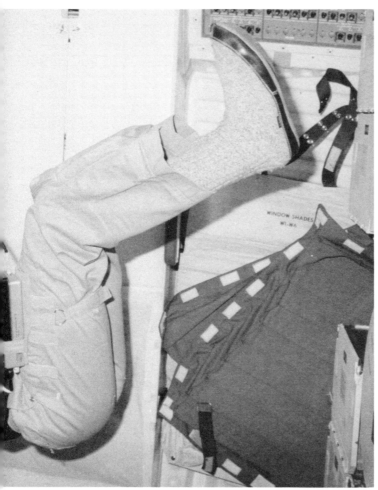

McNair plays an out-of-this-world solo during Mission 41-B. Noted for his conscientious, businesslike style, the astronaut surprised and delighted space fans with his high-spirited saxophone performance, a first in the history of space travel.

Mission 41-B was celebrated for its "first": McCandless and Stewart's "space walk." But another, although largely unpublicized, "first" had also taken place during the flight. McNair, usually the most serious and businesslike member of the crew, had boarded the shuttle with one piece of unauthorized equipment: his saxophone. As far as anyone knows, Ronald McNair was the first human being to play a saxophone solo in outer space.

Lake City celebrated its most famous son with a Ron McNair Day, featuring speeches, fireworks, speeches, a parade, and more speeches. Everybody in town—whites as well as blacks—seemed eager to reaffirm their lifetime affection for this handsome young astronaut. Lake City even renamed its main street, part of U.S. Highway 52: The section of the four-lane thoroughfare that runs through the town became Ronald E. McNair Boulevard. And in the town park—once off-limits to McNair and other blacks—the astronaut's boot prints were permanently embedded in a block of concrete.

While he was in Lake City, McNair paid a call on his pastor, the Reverend Michael Williams of Antioch Methodist Church. "It pleased me," said Williams later, "that Ron, who had to operate by and large in a white world, felt the need to have his own inner spirit refreshed by coming into contact with the joys of our particular ethnic tradition. He could have joined any white church in this city, but he chose a black church. I think that is significant."

Soon after the homecoming festivities, McNair returned to MIT, which had invited its celebrated alumnus to give a lecture about his experiences aboard the *Challenger*. The event had been organized by Michael Feld, McNair's former college adviser.

Invited to McNair's speech were not only MIT faculty members and students but pupils from all the high schools in the Boston area. McNair, who had delivered many lectures by this time, always made sure that young people, particularly minority students, received invitations to his talks.

One of McNair's old classmates, Bob di Jorio, had become director of the MIT news office. Commenting on his friend's appearance at the institute, di Jorio called McNair "a man of immense character who cared about people." Scientists, continued the school executive, "often never look to the left or right, but when you were with Ron, you knew you were with a real person who was interested in you."

Before speaking at MIT, McNair addressed the Massachusetts legislature on the subject of education.

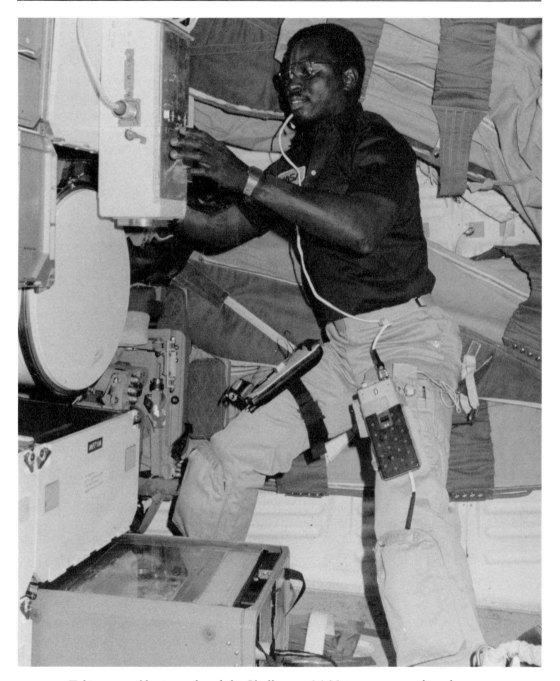

*Taking care of business aboard the Challenger, McNair prepares to adjust the mon-
odisperse latex reactor, a materials-processing experiment designed to make identical-
sized (monodisperse) latex particles. Strapped to the wall behind the astronaut are crew
members' sleep stations.*

He urged the lawmakers to raise teachers' salaries and to make a special effort to recruit first-rate teachers for inner-city areas. "Black minds and talent," he said, "have skills to control a spacecraft or scalpel with the same finesse and dexterity with which they control a basketball."

McNair entitled his MIT lecture "Being a Winner: Hanging It Over the Edge"—a phrase used by surfers and mountaineers. He challenged students to "step past our places of comfort . . . to walk over to the edge of our abilities and then move beyond that edge." The unknown, said McNair, "is mysterious. The unknown is frightening. But you can only become a winner if you are willing to walk over to the edge and dangle over it just a little bit."

McNair had certainly demonstrated his own willingness to take risks, but he still had to wait almost two years for his next ride into space. The 10th flight of the *Challenger*, Mission 51-L, was first scheduled for launch on December 23, 1985. It was to depart from the Kennedy Space Center; planned flight time was 6 days and 34 minutes, which would bring the craft back after its 97th orbit.

The original lift-off date was changed to January 23, 1986, because of a delay in an earlier-scheduled flight of the *Columbia*. Then, because of the work backlog that had piled up during the delay, NASA postponed the *Challenger* flight, first to January 25, then to the 26th. The weather forecast for the 26th, however, threatened bad conditions for a launch, and the date was changed to the 27th.

Mission 51-L had several objectives: One was to put a second tracking and data relay satellite (TDRS) into space. The first TDRS, launched by a *Challenger* crew in 1983, had failed to reach its proper orbit because of a malfunctioning booster rocket. A few months after its deployment, however, ground controllers managed to move the satellite into its proper orbit by using its attitude control thrusters, which are small steering rockets. The powerful TDRS is designed to collect data from information-gathering satellites and relay it to a central ground station at White Sands, New Mexico.

The *Challenger*'s cargo bay also contained the *Spartan-Halley* satellite, a 2,250-pound device built to photograph Halley's comet. English astronomer Edmond Halley had sighted the comet in 1682, calculated its orbit, and predicted it would return to earth's view about every 76 years. So it does. Through new and highly sophisticated equipment, astronomers now expected to get their best look yet at the great comet.

The *Spartan-Halley* was McNair territory. If things went according to plan, the shuttle's Remote Manipulator Arm would lift the satellite out of the cargo bay and release it outside the ship. In temporary free flight, the fully automated *Spartan-Halley* was to follow the orbiter while making photographic observations of the comet. After 22 orbits, the mechanical arm was to seize the satellite and return it to the cargo bay. Like the rest of the scientific world, McNair must have been wildly excited by the prospects of discovering new data about the fabled comet.

The general public, however, was even more excited about the presence on the *Challenger* of Christa McAuliffe. On day six of the mission, the New Hampshire schoolteacher was scheduled to broadcast two science lessons from the shuttle. Entitled "The Ultimate Field Trip," the first lesson would tell students about daily life in space. In the second lesson, McAuliffe planned to explain space-exploration methods and to discuss the possibilities of manufacturing new products in a gravity-free environment.

McAuliffe, of course, had not experienced the years of rigorous preparation for space travel undergone by her *Challenger* companions. Nevertheless, she had trained hard at the Johnson Space Center in Houston, and neither she nor NASA officials doubted her ability to make the flight. Mission 51-L had been preceded, after all, by 24 successful shuttle flights.

Although NASA and the public were confident, the space program had suffered several accidents. The worst had occurred on January 27, 1967: Astronauts Virgil Grissom, Edward White, and Roger Chaffee were killed when a flash fire engulfed their *Apollo* spacecraft at the Kennedy Space Center. The ground accident had horrified Americans, but it had not shaken their faith in NASA and its daring astronauts. In early 1986, the nation was proud of its space program and optimistic about its future.

On January 23, a roar of jets signaled the ritual of "astronaut arrival" at the Kennedy Space Center. Three T-38 trainer jets landed smartly in close formation on runway 15, followed by *NASA Two*, the executive jet. The ever-faithful press photographed the *Challenger*'s crew members as they came in from Houston for the next big ride.

Commander Scobee flew the lead plane, with mission specialist Ellison Onizuka aboard; the second jet held pilot Mike Smith and mission specialist Judy Resnik. With his usual athletic grace, specialist Ronald McNair jumped down from the third jet. After teacher Christa McAuliffe and civilian payload specialist Gregory Jarvis had emerged from the executive plane, the *Challenger* crew was complete.

Now all they had to do was get started.

On Monday morning, January 27, McNair awoke, saw that the sun was almost shining, and began to feel confident. Launch prospects seemed to be A-OK. Then trouble struck again. This time it was a stuck bolt on the handle of the outside hatch. Astronauts and spectators groaned. After spending more than an hour trying to loosen the stubborn bolt, a technician finally cut it with an ordinary hacksaw. "I would have gotten the hacksaw sooner," muttered Ed Corrigan, Christa McAuliffe's father. "I would have gotten my nail file," said his wife.

In any case, the bolt was free—but by then the weather had started acting up again. High winds began to blow across the launch site, a condition that would threaten an emergency landing. The mission was scrubbed for the day, and McNair and his frustrated comrades once again climbed out of the orbiter.

It began to look as though the *Challenger* would never get off the ground. ❧

8

THE FLIGHT
OF THE
CHALLENGER

————— ❧ —————

Tuesday, January 28, 1986, presented the awakening Ron McNair with a beautiful sight: blue skies over the Kennedy Space Center. At this hour—6:18 A.M.—there was no sign of rain, and the wind had died down. True, it was cold, unusually cold for Florida, even in January. But McNair knew the sun would warm the air as the day lengthened. Mission 51-L, it seemed, would fly at last.

McNair and his fellow astronauts attacked the traditional launch-day breakfast of steak and scrambled eggs. Then, shortly before 8 o'clock, they boarded a van and headed for the launch site. Crisply attired in their sky-blue space suits and polished black boots, the *Challenger's* seven-member crew waved and smiled at the crowd of photographers who trailed them. Even McNair, who normally disliked this part of the astronaut's preflight activities, beamed happily at the press.

Schoolchildren, watching from the visitors' stand at the Kennedy Space Center, cheer as the Challenger *streaks into the sky on January 28, 1986. The presence of schoolteacher Christa Mc-Auliffe made Mission 51-L particularly exciting for American youngsters.*

At pad 39B, the astronauts took an elevator to the "white room"—the chamber that led directly to the orbiter's hatch—and donned their harnesses and helmets. After suiting up, they entered the hatch, climbed the ladder to the orbiter, and strapped themselves into their reclining seats. The time was now 8:36 A.M. Lift-off was scheduled for 9:38.

Strapped in on the orbiter's flight deck were Scobee, occupying the commander's seat at the front left; Smith, on Scobee's right; Resnik in the aft-center seat; and Onizuka in the aft-right seat. On the *Challenger*'s middeck, below the flight deck, McNair occupied the left-hand seat. Jarvis sat on the right; McAuliffe, in the center.

Before McNair entered the spacecraft, the NASA quality-control technician briefed him on the hatch-locking mechanism. Because the lock had malfunctioned the day before, the ground crew would rely on McNair's visual inspection from inside to make sure the hatch was safely sealed. The astronaut quietly assured the technician that he knew what to look for.

As mission commander, Scobee was in charge of the shuttle from launch to reentry. Pilot Smith was second in command, qualified to take over the top job in an emergency.

As mission specialists, McNair, Resnik, and Onizuka were charged with carrying out the flight's assignments, which, on this trip, included operating the robot arm and tracking Halley's comet. Payload specialist Jarvis, representing the Hughes Aircraft Company, was to conduct experiments on the behavior of fluids under zero-gravity conditions; payload specialist McAuliffe would conduct her space-based classes.

The crew settled into their positions, checking their radio connections with Mission Control and exchanging banter. "My nose is freezing," remarked

Hawaiian-born Onizuka. "My butt is dead already," said Resnik. After the hatch was closed and sealed, McNair removed his helmet and carefully examined the locking pins as instructed. "I gave them a thumbs-up," he told Scobee. "They look good." It was now almost 9:00 A.M.

"Good morning, Judy," said astronaut support person (ASP) Sonny Carter. "Cowabunga," responded Judy Resnik cheerfully. "Good morning, Greg," said Carter. "Good morning, Billy Bob. How are you?" answered Greg Jarvis. "Fine. And you?" asked Carter. "Fannnnntastic!" Jarvis exclaimed. To Carter's "Good morning, Ron. How you doing?" McNair responded in his usual businesslike style: "Morning. Okay."

As the crew made their final adjustments, the ice team continued to remove ice from the launch platform. Meanwhile, NASA information officer Hugh Harris kept the thousands of spectators at the viewing site informed. At 11:28 A.M., Harris's voice boomed over the viewing stand.

"One minute away from picking up the count for the final nine minutes in the countdown," said Harris. "The countdown," he explained, "is simply a series of checks that people go through to ensure that everything is ready for flight. The countdown for a launch like 51-L is four volumes and more than 2,000 pages."

Listening intently on the roof of the launch control center were Scobee's wife and 21-year-old son; Smith's wife and three children; Onizuka's wife and two children; Resnik's mother and father; Jarvis's wife; McAuliffe's husband and two children; and McNair's wife and family. Cheryl McNair had arrived at the control center with her father, Harold Moore, 3-year-old Reggie, and 18-month-old Joy.

"T minus 8 minutes 30 seconds and counting," announced Harris. "All the flight recorders are turned on. Mission Control has turned on the auxiliary data system." (Flight data, explained Harris, would be sent back to mission control as the orbiter sped through the earth's atmosphere.)

The countdown continued. "T minus 5 minutes . . .' The crowd then heard launch control speaking directly to the *Challenger* crew: "Let's go for orbiter APU start." Mike Smith responded, "Performed APU start." (APUs are the auxiliary power units used to steer the orbiter, deploy its landing gear, and apply its brakes.) "Pilot Mike Smith," said Harris, "now flipping the three switches in the cockpit to start each of the three auxiliary power units. T minus 4 minutes 30 seconds and counting."

Cheryl McNair zipped up the children's jackets. It was very cold on the roof, but Reggie would enjoy waving good-bye to Daddy, and little Joy would one day understand what she had seen. Meanwhile, all along the Florida coastline, drivers tuned their radios, pulled their cars off the road, and watched for the *Challenger* to flash across the sky. At tracking stations around the world, technicians synchronized their antennae with the Florida countdown sequence.

"T minus 3 minutes and 45 seconds," said Harris. "Orbiter ground-support equipment power bus has been turned off, and the vehicle is now on internal power."

Less than two minutes from launch, the crew was still trading jokes. "Okay, there goes the lox [liquid oxygen] arm," said Smith. "Goes the beanie cap," said Scobee, referring to the tip of the arm on the external tank. "Doesn't it go the other way?" Onizuka chimed in. The astronauts roared with laughter. "God, I hope not, Ellison," said Smith.

At T minus 6 seconds, all 3 of the orbiter's main engines were operating at 100 percent of their power. Over the ear-splitting din of the engines, McNair could hear Scobee's calm voice. "Three at a hundred," he said.

McNair (right), Christa McAuliffe (left), and Gregory Jarvis try out their flight position in the simulator middeck. By the time the Challenger blasted off, McAuliffe and Jarvis had switched seats; McNair, responsible for the tricky hatch-locking mechanism, remained in his position next to the hatch.

"Lift-off!" shouted Harris over the loudspeaker. The *Challenger* roared into the blue Florida sky.

The noise was deafening. But all those thousands of switches and buttons and machine parts and computers and bolts and flashing lights were working perfectly. In a brilliant flash of light, followed by billowing clouds of white smoke, the *Challenger* sliced through the atmosphere. Awestruck spectators cheered, screamed, applauded, and hugged each other.

Seven seconds after lift-off, Scobee prepared for his first maneuver, rotating the *Challenger* to its ascent attitude, facing the earth. "Roll program [the rotation move] confirmed," crackled the space center's loudspeaker. "*Challenger* now heading downrange. Engines beginning to throttle down to 94 percent. . . . Three engines running normally. Three good fuel cells. Three good APUs. Velocity 2,257 feet per second [1,538 miles per hour]. Altitude 4.3 nautical miles. Downrange distance, 3 nautical miles. Engines throttling up. Three engines now at 104 percent."

"Go, you mother!" shouted an exuberant Mike Smith.

Three seconds later, McNair and his colleagues felt the first stiff winds hit the *Challenger*. The spacecraft shuddered and swayed under the tremendous force. McNair heard Smith say, "Looks like we've got a lot of wind up here today." Scobee, apparently unconcerned, said, "Yeah."

At T plus 1 minute, 2 seconds, Scobee reported, "Thirty-five thousand [feet in altitude]. Going through one point five [one and one-half times the speed of sound, or almost 1,100 miles per hour]."

At T plus 1 minute, 7 seconds, ground control ordered Scobee to "go at throttle up [continue at full throttle]." Three seconds later, Scobee responded, "Roger, go at throttle up." The *Challenger* was now streaking upward at 2,900 feet per second; it had reached an altitude of 50,800 feet.

At T plus 1:13, Mike Smith said, "Uhh . . . oh . . ." It was the last sound recorded by the crew of the Challenger.

At first, no one—not the crew, not the spectators, mission control, the television audience, not even the computer—had noticed, but at T plus 10 seconds—73 seconds into the flight—a small orange flame had erupted from a joint on the right-hand solid rocket booster. As the spacecraft was hit by the most violent winds ever encountered on a mission, the flame blossomed into a tremendous fireball enveloped by a seething, fiery cloud.

Suddenly, out of the flame-streaked cloud, the Challenger's twin rocket boosters shot away into twin arcs. Seconds later, the boosters exploded, destroyed by a radio signal from the air force range safety officer. Then the huge external tank disintegrated, consumed by its own flaming fuel.

The orbiter carrying the seven Challenger astronauts disappeared from view. On the ground, spectators gazed upward in disbelief, not sure what they had witnessed but knowing something had gone terribly wrong. The moment of stunned silence was broken by Mike Smith's nine-year-old daughter, Erin. "Daddy! Daddy!" she cried out, "I want you, Daddy! You promised nothing would happen!"

Over the loudspeakers came the unemotional voice of Steve Nesbitt at the Johnson Space Center in Houston. "Flight controllers are looking very carefully at the situation," he said. "Obviously a major malfunction." Ground control had lost touch with the Challenger: "We have no downlink," reported Nesbitt. Seconds later, speaking in the same carefully controlled tone, he said, "We have a report from the flight-dynamics officer that the vehicle has exploded. The flight director confirms that."

As a Kennedy Space Center official gazes upward, the Challenger disappears in a dense cloud of smoke. Until this point, neither onlookers nor mission control had detected anything amiss, but apparently Michael Smith had; a later review of flight-deck tapes revealed the pilot's last words: "Uhh . . . oh . . ."

The *Challenger* had plummeted from the sky, dropping 65,000 feet in 2 minutes, 45 seconds, and slamming into the Atlantic Ocean at a speed of 204 miles per hour.

In New Hampshire's Concord High School, Christa McAuliffe's students watched the explosion in horror. Some reacted with stunned silence; others wept and threw their arms around each other. "Someone they admired and loved has been taken away," said the school's principal later. "They have learned that nothing in this life is certain."

At 4:30 P.M., 5 hours after the *Challenger* disappeared, Johnson Space Center director Jesse Moore spoke to reporters at Cape Canaveral. "It is with deep, heartfelt sorrow that I address you here this afternoon," he said, his voice trembling. "At 11:30 A.M. this morning, the space program experienced a national tragedy with the explosion of the space shuttle *Challenger* approximately a minute and a half after launch from here at the Kennedy Space Center. I regret that I have to report that based on a very preliminary search of the ocean where *Challenger* impacted this morning—these searches have not revealed any evidence that the crew of *Challenger* survived."

The unthinkable had become real. Linked by television, millions of people had actually witnessed the fiery death of seven gallant men and women. Shocked Americans reacted with an outpouring of sorrow and sympathy for the astronauts' families. As a columnist for the *Orlando Sentinel* put it, "The relatives are now left to cope with the sight that has linked strangers in grief: Seven people at the pinnacle of their lives, riding a symbol of national achievement in a disintegrating fireball."

Former astronaut Michael Collins called the *Challenger* seven "a microcosm of American society." Watching their spacecraft "being blown to bits," he said, "was like witnessing a tiny, but vital, piece of this country being destroyed."

Flags flew at half-mast across America. In silent tribute to the fallen astronauts, millions of citizens switched on their car lights, left their front-porch lamps lighted, and pointed flashlights into the sky. In Los Angeles, the Memorial Coliseum's Olympic torch was relighted; in New York City, the Empire State Building shut off its blazing floodlights. In towns and cities all over the United States, residents put up hand-lettered signs with such messages as We Salute Our Heroes. God Bless Them All.

On January 31, three days after the disaster, President Ronald Reagan and his wife, Nancy, attended a memorial service for the *Challenger* crew at the Johnson Space Center. Also present were 10,000 others—NASA employees, politicians, and relatives of the astronauts. The mourners, many of them holding small American flags, listened as the air force band played funeral hymns and four T-38 jets—the aircraft in which the astronauts had trained for their last mission—thundered overhead. Nancy Reagan cradled Joy McNair as the president spoke.

"The sacrifice of your loved ones has stirred the soul of our nation, and through the pain, our hearts have been opened to a profound truth," Reagan told the astronaut's families. "We learned again that this America was built on heroism and noble sacrifice. It was built on men and women like our seven star voyagers, who answered a call beyond duty."

Ending his tribute, the president said, "We remember Dick Scobee, the commander. . . . We remember Michael Smith, who earned enough medals as a combat pilot to cover his chest. We remember Judith Resnik, known as J.R. to her friends. We remember Ellison Onizuka, who, as a child running barefoot through the coffee fields and macadamia groves of Hawaii, dreamed of someday traveling to the moon.

Their faces etched with disbelief and horror, spectators watch the fiery destruction of Mission 51-L. Minutes later, the Challenger screamed into the ocean at the speed of 204 miles per hour. There were no survivors.

At Cape Canaveral, an empty launchpad and a half-masted American flag bear silent witness to a nation's grief. Speaking at a memorial service for the fallen heroes, President Ronald Reagan said, "Dick, Mike, Judy, El, Ron, Greg, and Christa—your families and your country mourn your passing. We bid you good-bye, but we will never forget you."

"We remember Ronald McNair, who said he learned perseverance in the cotton fields of South Carolina. We remember Gregory Jarvis—on that ill-fated flight he was carrying with him a flag of his university in Buffalo. We remember Christa Mc-Auliffe, who captured the imagination of an entire nation. . . . Today we promise Dick Scobee and his crew that their dream lives on; that the future they worked so to build will become reality. Dick, Mike, Judy, El, Ron, Greg, and Christa—your families and your country mourn your passing. We bid you good-bye, but we will never forget you."

McNair's alma mater, North Carolina Agriculture and Technical State University, held its own memorial service. Speaking at the ceremony was another of the school's celebrated graduates, civil rights leader Jesse Jackson. After a choir had sung a group of traditional spirituals, Jackson told hundreds of weeping listeners that "to appreciate Ronald McNair, one needs to understand Lake City, South Carolina, a town several miles deeper than the country. Ron and his two brothers picked cotton and cropped tobacco to help their family. But from that place, God chose a laser physicist to defy the odds of oppression." McNair, said Jackson, "belongs to the ages now."

Messages of sympathy came from all over the world. Soviet Union leader Mikhail Gorbachev said, "We share the feelings of sorrow in connection with the tragic death of the crew of the space shuttle *Challenger*. We express our condolences to their families and to the people of the United States."

The nation's next order of business was an investigation of the disaster. Exactly what had happened? Who was at fault? A week after the event, Reagan created the Presidential Commission on the Space Shuttle *Challenger* Accident. Four months later, after examining every aspect of the fatal flight, the commission would release its report on the shocking tragedy.

Salvors prepare to store a section of the Challenger at Cape Canaveral. Hoping to discover the flaw that destroyed the shuttle and its 7 occupants, NASA mounted the greatest marine salvage effort in history, eventually recovering about 30 percent of the spacecraft. Investigation of the fragments revealed that faulty O-rings had led to the disaster.

Meanwhile, NASA, assisted by the U.S. Coast Guard, the navy, the air force, the National Transportation Safety Board, and private contractors, began the most extensive marine salvage operation in history. Searching both the surface and the bottom of the ocean, salvagers collected about 30 percent of the *Challenger*'s structure in three months. All the material was loaded on ships, brought to Port Canaveral, then trucked to a special hangar on the cape. To learn how and why the shuttle broke up, investigators examined every shred of debris, then reassembled as many of the pieces as possible.

On March 8, after hundreds of thousands of work hours, salvagers found the *Challenger*'s crew compartment. It was submerged in 90 feet of water, some 16 miles off the Florida coast. A month later, divers located the remains of the seven astronauts who had perished with their spacecraft. After identification, they were released to their families. Ronald McNair was buried in his hometown.

The presidential commission's report suggested that the *Challenger* crew survived the fireball. They had apparently died soon afterward, either of decompression in the module or as a result of their impact with the ocean. In any case, most authorities believe that the astronauts could have been conscious for no more than 15 seconds after the explosion, which carried the module to an altitude of 65,000 feet before it dropped into the sea.

In its June 1986 report, the presidential commission concluded that "the cause of the *Challenger* accident was the failure of the pressure seal in the aft field joint of the right solid rocket motor." By "pressure seal," the commission meant one of the solid rocket booster's O-rings. These small (one-quarter inch in diameter), flexible rubber rings seal the joints between the booster's steel segments.

The *Challenger* launch had taken place in cold weather—the coldest of any launch in NASA's history—which had caused the rubber rings to lose their resilience. The failure of the rings had allowed flames to escape the booster and burn through the skin of the external fuel tanks.

The decision to launch the *Challenger*, said the commission, had been "flawed." Engineers from Morton Thiokol, the company that built the booster rockets, had suspected that the O-rings might not stand up to cold temperatures. They had suggested that NASA delay the launch until the weather warmed up, but NASA officials were eager to get the spacecraft aloft. When NASA disputed the engineers' recommendations, they withdrew their objections to the launch.

"If the decision-makers had known all the facts," concluded the commission's report, "it is highly unlikely that they would have decided to launch . . . on January 28, 1986." But the commission also expressed faith in NASA's future. "The agency constitutes a national resource that plays a critical role in space exploration and development," said the report. "It also provides a symbol of national pride and leadership. The commission applauds NASA's spectacular achievements of the past and anticipates impressive achievements to come."

During the next two years, NASA went about its work of reorganization and redirection. The faulty O-rings were redesigned and some 400 modifications, all of them aimed at preventing another *Challenger* catastrophe, were incorporated into the shuttle. On September 29, 1988, the shuttle *Discovery*, its module containing five astronauts, stood on the launchpad at the Kennedy Space Center. The nation held its breath. But all went well: mission accomplished. The space shuttle and the U.S. space program were back in business.

But the tragedy of the *Challenger* and its crew will never be forgotten. Families and fellow citizens have

After a funeral service in Lake City, South Carolina, Cheryl McNair follows the casket containing her husband's remains. Grieving friends and relatives, including Ronald McNair's brother Carl, Jr. (right), wear lapel pins imprinted with the astronaut's likeness.

commemorated the astronauts in many ways. Craters on the moon, for example, were named for each of them. In December 1986, MIT dedicated the Ronald E. McNair Building, a huge campus structure housing MIT's Center for Space Research and part of its aeronautics and astronautics department. Reginald McNair, then four years old, unveiled the dedication engraved on the stone wall in the lobby.

The carved words read: Ronald E. McNair Building, Named in Memory of Ronald Erwin McNair, Ph.D. 1976, Scientist, Astronaut, Alumnus. Below was a quote from McNair, expressing his thoughts when he first viewed the earth from space: "My wish is that we would allow this planet to be the beautiful oasis that she is, and allow ourselves to live more in the peace that she generates."

After the unveiling, a number of MIT officials talked about McNair. The astronaut, said MIT chairman David Saxton, "truly symbolized" the MIT motto, *mens et manus*, Latin for "mind and hand." The institute's president, Paul Gray, called McNair "a builder of bridges—bridges between people.

"A black man who grew up in a segregated society, Ron used his talents and his teachings—in science, in religion, in the arts, in athletics—to form friendships and connections with many people from many races and cultures," continued Gray. "In forming these bridges, he was able to retain and, indeed, to celebrate his own cultural identity.

"What else is there to say about this man?" asked Gray, his voice cracking with emotion. "Say that he was an *achiever*. Ron was not content with halfway measures, with average goals, with median achievements. . . . He stuck to his dreams, and he brought to each part of his life an indomitable spirit and a shining belief in his own capacity to succeed. He held the promise of future leadership for a nation that has too few heroes. . . . Ron McNair is, was, a real live hero."

Also speaking at the MIT ceremony was McNair's old friend and fellow black astronaut, Colonel Charles F. Bolden, Jr. Looking into the future, Bolden said, "I see young men and young women coming to MIT and saying, 'I want to go where Ron McNair went. I want to go where Ron McNair dared. I want to go where Ron McNair chose to start his life taking risks.' "

Bolden recalled that McNair had often quoted the words of educator Horace Mann: "Be ashamed to die until you've won some victory for humanity." McNair "won a lot of victories for humanity," said Bolden. "Ron was the best that he could be."

A few months later, the Davis Planetarium in Jackson, Mississippi, commissioned a larger-than-life portrait of McNair and renamed its theater for him. And in Lake City, South Carolina, Carver High

School became Ronald E. McNair Junior High School, honoring the memory of number 21, the 145-pound linebacker whose coach once called him a "total football player."

Cheryl McNair, who continued to live in Houston, attended many of the dedications with her children. She told one interviewer that she hoped people would remember the *Challenger* disaster not only as the nation's worst space tragedy but "as a time when the world came together in one vein, in the spirit of love." The most fitting memorial for her husband, she said, is the inspiration he gave young people. "He stressed progress and the need to motivate youths," she pointed out. "He believed in encouraging young people to persevere to excel in whatever they set out to do."

Indeed, after he joined NASA, the quiet, unassuming McNair had jumped at the chance to talk to students across the nation. He visited schools from New York to California, encouraging promising black students to enroll in graduate science programs. Everywhere he went, McNair was surrounded by admiring young people who asked for his autograph. He always signed his name, then added his personal creed: "Be your best!"

McNair often told his young audiences a story about an eagle who had been raised with chickens and who had come to believe he *was* a chicken. "The chickens had wings but could not fly," he said. "They lived together but did not protect each other. Then, one day, the eagle saw a flock of eagles fly by."

The young eagle, continued McNair, "felt a power he had never felt before, felt a pride he had never experienced. He ran across the barnyard, flapped his wings, and left the chickens on the ground, soaring over the trees and mountaintops." At this point in his story, McNair would raise his voice. "*Black students, minority students,*" he would

Cheryl, Joy, and Reginald Mc-Nair, flanked by MIT president Paul Gray and his wife, Priscilla, attend a 1986 ceremony dedicating MIT's Ronald E. McNair Building. The astronaut "held the promise of future leadership for a nation that has too few heroes," said Gray. "Ron McNair is, was, a real live hero."

shout. "You're not chickens. You're eagles! You don't belong on the ground. You're not dumb. You're not ugly. Stretch your wings and fly to the sky!"

In 1984, McNair's boyhood friend Dozier Montgomery, then teaching fifth graders in South Carolina, suggested that his pupils write a letter to McNair and ask about their own chances for a space career. Responding to their letter, McNair noted that many astronauts had attended large schools in major cities. However, he said, "let the fact that there is one from

Lake City, S.C., serve as a lesson to you that it doesn't matter where you come from." Concluding the letter, he offered the youngsters some advice. "Whether or not you reach your goals in life," he said, "depends entirely on how well you prepare for them and how badly you want them."

McNair's words came from the heart. He was born poor, brought up in a small southern town, and educated in segregated schools, but he never accepted second best. In his 35 years, McNair accomplished more than most people accomplish in a full life span.

A Star Scout, McNair graduated from high school and college with high honors. At 21, he was named a Ford Foundation fellow; at 24, a fellow of the National Fellowship Fund and a NATO fellow. In 1975, he won the Omega Psi Phi Scholar of the Year Award.

McNair became a member of the American Association for the Advancement of Science, the American Physical Society (APS), the APS Committee on Minorities in Physics, the American Optical Society, the Board of Trustees of the North Carolina School of Science and Mathematics, and the MIT Corporation Visiting Committee.

A visiting lecturer on physics at Texas Southern University in Houston, McNair received an honorary doctorate of laws from North Carolina A&T State University and honorary doctorates in science from Morris College in South Carolina and the University of South Carolina.

Capping his brief but brilliant career, McNair became one of the elite handful of Americans chosen to serve their nation as astronauts. As MIT's Paul Gray put it, "He set extraordinary standards for himself—higher than anyone else would dare set for him—and then met and exceeded those standards." Never daunted by the odds, quiet but fiercely determined, McNair achieved even more than he had dreamed of. Aiming high, he reached the stars. ✺

CHRONOLOGY

1950   Born Ronald Erwin McNair on October 21 in Lake City, South Carolina

1967   Graduates as valedictorian from Carver High School in Lake City

1971   Graduates magna cum laude from North Carolina Agricultural and Technical State University; named Ford Foundation fellow

1976   Receives doctorate in physics from Massachusetts Institute of Technology; marries Cheryl Moore; joins Hughes Research Laboratories in Malibu, California, as a staff physicist

1978   Accepted by the National Aeronautics and Space Administration (NASA) for astronaut candidate program

1979   Completes one-year astronaut training program

1984   Makes first spaceflight, aboard the shuttle *Challenger*

1986   Makes second spaceflight and dies in *Challenger* explosion on January 28

FURTHER READING

Branley, Franklyn M. *From Sputnik to Space Shuttles: Into the New Space Age.* New York: Crowell, 1986.

Cohen, Daniel, and Susan Cohen. *Heroes of the Challenger.* New York: Archway, 1986.

Collins, Michael. *Carrying the Fire: An Astronaut's Journeys.* New York: Farrar, Straus & Giroux, 1974.

————. *Liftoff: The Story of America's Adventure in Space.* New York: Grove Press, 1988.

Crouch, Tom. *The National Aeronautics and Space Administration.* New York: Chelsea House, 1990.

Hirsch, Richard, and Joseph Trento. *The National Aeronautics and Space Administration.* New York: Praeger, 1973.

Lewis, Richard S. *Challenger: The Final Voyage.* New York: Columbia University Press, 1988.

McDougall, Walter A. *Heavens and the Earth: A Political History of the Space Age.* New York: Basic Books, 1985.

"The Problems of Living in Space." In *Science Now*, edited by James Harrison. New York: Arco, 1984.

Smith, Robert W. *The Space Telescope.* New York: Cambridge University Press, 1990.

Trento, Joseph J. *Prescription for Disaster: From the Glory of Apollo to the Betrayal of the Shuttle.* New York: Crown, 1987.

We Seven: By the Astronauts Themselves. New York: Simon & Schuster, 1962.

INDEX

PICTURE CREDITS

———— ❧ ————

CORINNE NADEN, a graduate of New York University, served four years in the U.S. Navy, editing a weekly newspaper and writing training-film scripts. A former children's book editor, she is the author of 15 books for children and coauthor of 3 books for children's librarians and teachers.

NATHAN IRVIN HUGGINS is W.E.B. Du Bois Professor of History and Director of the W.E.B. Du Bois Institute for Afro-American Research at Harvard University. He previously taught at Columbia University. Professor Huggins is the author of numerous books, including *Black Odyssey: The Afro-American Ordeal in Slavery, The Harlem Renaissance,* and *Slave and Citizen: The Life of Frederick Douglass.*